SAMOA ISLAND TRAVEL GUIDE 2024

"The complete insider guide to exploring the best of Samoa island beaches, cuisines, insider tips, outdoor activities, adventures, shopping, museums, arts, festivals and events, hidden gems"

Mercy Davis

TABLE OF CONTENTS

INTRODUCTION

As I stepped off the plane and felt the warm embrace of Samoa's tropical breeze, I knew I was about to embark on a journey like no other. The islands of Samoa, with their unspoiled beauty and rich cultural heritage, promised an adventure that would stay with me forever. This travel guide is my heartfelt invitation to you to experience the magic of Samoa firsthand.

I remember my first glimpse of the pristine beaches, where the turquoise waters kissed the powdery white sands. The vibrant colors of the island's flora and the harmonious sounds of nature instantly captivated me. It was as if the hustle and bustle of my everyday life had melted away, leaving only a sense of peace and wonder.

During my stay, I had the privilege of visiting traditional Samoan villages, where I was warmly welcomed by the locals. Their stories, filled with ancestral wisdom and a deep connection to the land, left an indelible mark on my heart. Sharing meals with families, partaking in communal feasts, and learning about the customs that have been passed down through generations were experiences that opened my eyes to the true spirit of Samoa.

One particularly unforgettable day was when I visited the To Sua Ocean Trench. As I climbed down the ladder into the crystal-clear waters, I felt a thrill of excitement mixed with a touch of fear. But as I floated in that natural wonder, surrounded by lush greenery and the sound of waves echoing in the distance, I felt a profound connection to the natural world. It was moments like these that made me realize why Samoa is often referred to as the Heart of Polynesia.

Samoa isn't just a destination; it's a feeling. It's the warmth of the people, the rhythm of the daily life, and the breathtaking landscapes that make you feel alive and grounded at the same time. Whether you're seeking adventure, relaxation, or a deep cultural immersion, Samoa offers it all.

In this guide, I will share with you everything I discovered about Samoa, from the best times to visit and essential travel tips to hidden gems and must-see attractions. My goal is to equip you with all the information you need to have an amazing and unforgettable experience. I'll take you through the bustling markets of Apia, guide you to the serene beaches of Lalomanu, and introduce you to the sacred sites that hold the stories of this incredible land.

As you turn the pages of this book, I hope you'll feel the same excitement and curiosity I did when I first set foot on these enchanting islands. Samoa has so much to offer, and I'm thrilled to share its wonders with you. So pack your bags, open your heart, and get ready to explore the paradise that is Samoa. Welcome to your next great adventure!

Why Visit Samoa in 2024?

As we step into 2024, Samoa remains one of the Pacific's best-kept secrets, offering an unparalleled blend of natural beauty, rich culture, and genuine hospitality. Whether you're a seasoned traveler or planning your first tropical getaway, Samoa has something extraordinary to offer this year. Here are a few compelling reasons to make Samoa your travel destination in 2024.

Unspoiled Natural Beauty

Samoa's landscape is a feast for the eyes. From the dramatic coastlines and pristine beaches to lush rainforests and cascading waterfalls, the islands are a nature lover's paradise. The famous To Sua Ocean Trench, with its crystal-clear waters and stunning surroundings, continues to be a bucket-list destination. Visiting in 2024 means you can witness these natural wonders without the overcrowding that often accompanies more well-known destinations.

Cultural Immersion

Samoa is steeped in tradition and culture, and 2024 is the perfect time to immerse yourself in its rich heritage. The local communities are eager to share their way of life, offering visitors a chance to experience traditional Samoan hospitality firsthand. Engage in a fiafia night, where you can enjoy traditional music, dance, and a feast that showcases the best of Samoan cuisine. Exploring the villages and meeting the locals will give you a deeper appreciation for the island's unique cultural tapestry.

Sustainable Tourism Initiatives

In 2024, Samoa is focusing more on sustainable tourism, ensuring that the beauty and integrity of the islands are preserved for future generations. As a visitor, you can participate in eco-friendly activities and support local businesses that are committed to conservation and sustainability. Whether it's staying in eco-lodges, participating in beach clean-ups, or engaging in community-based tourism projects, you can enjoy your holiday knowing you're making a positive impact.

Exciting Events and Festivals

2024 promises an array of vibrant events and festivals that celebrate Samoan culture, art, and sports. The Teuila Festival, held annually in September, is a highlight, offering a week of traditional performances, arts and crafts, and culinary delights. Additionally, Samoa will host several international sporting events, providing a thrilling experience for sports enthusiasts and a chance to witness the athletic prowess of the Samoan people.

Adventure Awaits

For those seeking adventure, Samoa is a playground of activities. The islands offer world-class snorkeling and diving sites teeming with marine life. Surfing enthusiasts can catch some of the best waves in the Pacific, while hikers can explore scenic trails that lead to hidden waterfalls and panoramic views. The year 2024 introduces new guided tours and adventure packages, making it easier than ever to explore the untouched beauty of Samoa.

Authentic Experiences

One of the most appealing aspects of visiting Samoa in 2024 is the opportunity to have authentic, off-the-beaten-path experiences. Unlike many overcrowded tourist destinations, Samoa offers a more intimate and personal travel experience. You can find secluded beaches, enjoy a picnic under the shade of a coconut tree, and explore quaint villages where time seems to stand still.

Welcoming Atmosphere

The heart and soul of Samoa are its people. Known for their warmth and friendliness, the Samoans make every visitor feel at home. Whether you're staying at a luxury resort or a family-run guesthouse, the hospitality you'll receive is second to none. This welcoming atmosphere makes Samoa a perfect destination for solo travelers, couples, and families alike.

In conclusion, 2024 is an ideal year to visit Samoa, with its blend of natural wonders, cultural richness, and a strong commitment to sustainability. Whether you're seeking relaxation, adventure, or a deep cultural connection, Samoa offers a unique and unforgettable experience. So, pack your bags and get ready to explore the paradise that awaits you in the heart of the Pacific. Welcome to Samoa, where every moment is a treasure waiting to be discovered.

Quick Facts About Samoa

Location:
Samoa is located in the South Pacific Ocean, about halfway between Hawaii and New Zealand. It comprises two main islands, Upolu and Savai'i, along with several smaller islands.

Capital:
Apia, situated on the island of Upolu, is the capital and largest city of Samoa. It serves as the main hub for government, commerce, and culture.

Population:
Samoa has a population of approximately 200,000 people, with the majority residing on the island of Upolu.

Language:
The official languages are Samoan and English. Samoan is widely spoken and used in daily communication, while English is commonly used in business and government affairs.

Currency:
The Samoan currency is the tala (WST). Credit cards are accepted in larger establishments, but it's advisable to carry cash for transactions in rural areas and smaller businesses.

Time   Zone:

Samoa operates on Samoa Standard Time (SST), which is UTC+13. The country observes daylight saving time, moving one hour forward during the summer months.

Climate:

Samoa enjoys a tropical climate with warm temperatures year-round. The dry season runs from May to October, while the wet season occurs from November to April, often bringing heavy rain and occasional cyclones.

Religion:

Christianity is the predominant religion in Samoa, with various denominations present, including Congregationalists, Catholics, Methodists, and more. Religion plays a significant role in Samoan culture and daily life.

Government:

Samoa is a parliamentary democracy with a Head of State (O le Ao o le Malo) and a Prime Minister who leads the government. The legislative body is the Fono, consisting of two chambers.

Economy:

The economy of Samoa is primarily based on agriculture, tourism, and remittances from Samoans living abroad. Key agricultural products include coconut, taro, bananas, and cocoa.

Culture:

Samoan culture, or fa'a Samoa, emphasizes community, family, and respect for elders. Traditional customs, music, dance, and crafts are integral to daily life and celebrated through various festivals and ceremonies.

National Symbols:

- **Flag:** The Samoan flag features a red field with a blue rectangle in the top left corner, containing the Southern Cross constellation in white.

- **Emblem:** The national emblem includes a shield with a coconut palm and a cross, symbolizing Christianity, surrounded by traditional Samoan motifs.

Key Attractions:

- To Sua Ocean Trench: A stunning natural swimming hole on Upolu.

- Lalomanu Beach: A beautiful white-sand beach ideal for relaxation and water activities.

- Robert Louis Stevenson Museum: The former home of the famous author, now a museum.

- Savai'i: Known for its rugged beauty, lava fields, and traditional villages.

- Apia: Offers markets, cultural sites, and vibrant local life.

Transportation:
Samoa has a reliable network of buses, taxis, and rental cars available for getting around. Inter-island ferries connect Upolu and Savai'i, making travel between the islands convenient.

Health **and** **Safety:**
Travelers are advised to take standard health precautions, including vaccinations and drinking bottled or boiled water. Samoa is generally safe, but it's wise to stay informed about local conditions and follow safety guidelines.

These quick facts provide a snapshot of what makes Samoa a unique and inviting destination. With its warm climate, rich culture, and stunning landscapes, Samoa is ready to welcome you to an unforgettable adventure.

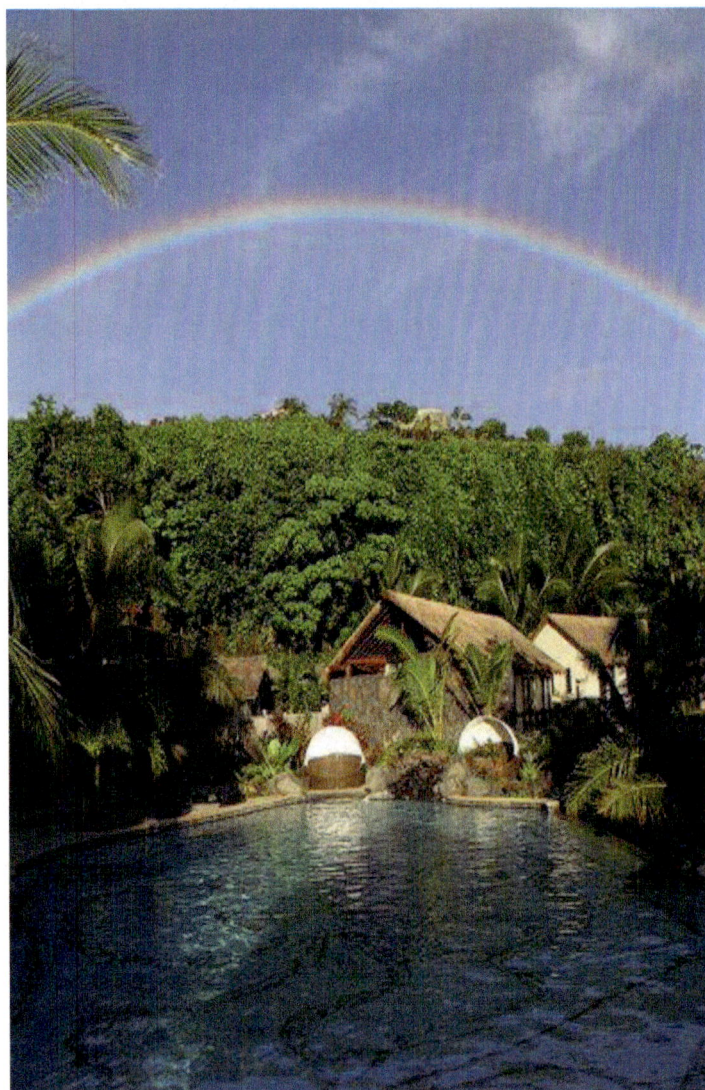

PLANNING YOUR TRIP

Traveling to Samoa is an adventure filled with natural beauty, rich culture, and warm hospitality. As you plan your journey, consider several key factors to ensure a smooth and enjoyable experience. This comprehensive guide covers the best time to visit, entry requirements and visa information, flights and transportation, currency and budgeting, and travel insurance.

Best Time to Visit

Climate and Seasons

Samoa enjoys a tropical climate, with warm temperatures year-round. The country experiences two main seasons: the dry season and the wet season. Understanding the climate can help you decide the best time for your visit.

- **Dry Season (May to October):** This is the most popular time to visit Samoa, as the weather is generally sunny and dry. Temperatures range from 24°C to 30°C (75°F to 86°F), making it ideal for beach activities, sightseeing, and outdoor adventures. The dry season coincides with Samoa's peak tourist season, so it's wise to book accommodations and tours in advance.

- **Wet Season (November to April):** During this period, Samoa experiences higher humidity, frequent rain showers, and occasional tropical cyclones. While the wet season can bring heavy rainfall, it also means lush landscapes and fewer tourists. If you prefer a quieter experience and don't mind occasional rain, this could be a good time to explore Samoa.

Festivals and Events

Samoa hosts several vibrant festivals throughout the year, adding cultural richness to your visit.

- **Teuila Festival (September):** One of Samoa's biggest cultural events, the Teuila Festival features traditional dance, music, arts, and culinary competitions. It's an excellent opportunity to immerse yourself in Samoan culture.

- **Independence Day (June 1st):** Celebrations include parades, traditional performances, and sports events, reflecting the national pride and unity of the Samoan people.

Considerations for Families and Special Interests

For families, visiting during school holidays in the dry season ensures good weather for beach outings and family-friendly activities. For those interested in surfing or diving, specific times within the dry season may offer the best conditions. Consulting local surf or dive schools can provide insights on the optimal months for these activities.

Entry Requirements and Visa Information

Passports and Visa

Visitors to Samoa must have a valid passport with at least six months of validity from the date of entry. Entry requirements can vary depending on your nationality.

- **Visa-Free Entry:** Citizens of several countries, including Australia, New Zealand, the United States, and most European Union countries, do not require a visa for stays up to 60 days. A valid passport, return or onward ticket, and proof of sufficient funds are required.

- **Visa on Arrival:** Nationals of other countries can obtain a visa on arrival, typically valid for 60 days. You will need to show a valid passport, a return or onward ticket, and proof of sufficient funds.

- **Extended Stays:** For stays longer than 60 days, visitors must apply for an extension through the Immigration Office in Apia. Extensions are granted on a case-by-case basis and may require additional documentation.

Health Requirements

Travelers are advised to check health and vaccination requirements before departure. Although no vaccinations are mandatory for entry into Samoa, it's recommended to be up-to-date on routine vaccines. Depending on your travel history, a Yellow Fever vaccination certificate may be required if you are arriving from a country where Yellow Fever is present.

Flights and Transportation

Getting to Samoa

Samoa is accessible via international flights, primarily arriving at Faleolo International Airport (APW) near Apia on the island of Upolu. Several airlines operate flights to Samoa from major hubs in the Pacific region.

- **From Australia and New Zealand:** Direct flights are available from cities like Sydney, Brisbane, and Auckland, with airlines such as Air New Zealand and Samoa Airways offering regular services.

- **From the United States:** Travelers from the United States typically connect through Auckland or other Pacific hubs. Hawaiian Airlines provides a direct flight from Honolulu to Samoa.

Domestic Travel

Once in Samoa, domestic travel between the main islands of Upolu and Savai'i is straightforward.

- **Ferries:** Regular ferry services operate between Mulifanua Wharf on Upolu and Salelologa Wharf on Savai'i. The ferry ride takes approximately 90 minutes.

It's advisable to check the schedule in advance, as weather conditions can affect service.

- **Domestic Flights:** For a quicker option, Samoa Airways offers short flights between Faleolo International Airport and Maota Airport on Savai'i. The flight duration is about 20 minutes.

Getting Around the Islands

Traveling within the islands is convenient, with various transportation options available.

- **Taxis:** Taxis are widely available and reasonably priced. It's recommended to agree on the fare before starting your journey, as taxis in Samoa do not use meters.

- **Buses:** Public buses are a colorful and economical way to travel, especially on Upolu. While buses do not run on a strict schedule, they offer an authentic way to experience local life. Buses generally operate from early morning until late afternoon.

- **Rental Cars:** Renting a car provides the most flexibility for exploring at your own pace. Several rental agencies operate in Apia and at Faleolo International Airport. An international driving permit is required, which can be obtained from the Ministry of Works, Transport, and Infrastructure in Apia.

Currency and Budgeting

Currency

The currency in Samoa is the Samoan Tala (WST), often abbreviated as ST or T. It's important to have local currency on hand, especially when traveling to rural areas where credit card acceptance may be limited.

- **Exchange Rates:** Exchange rates can fluctuate, so it's advisable to check current rates before exchanging money. Currency exchange services are available at the airport, banks, and major hotels.

- **ATMs and Credit Cards:** ATMs are widely available in Apia and other major towns. Visa and MasterCard are commonly accepted, but it's prudent to carry cash for small purchases and in more remote areas. Some ATMs may charge a fee for international cards.

Budgeting

Samoa offers a range of accommodation and dining options to suit different budgets.

- **Accommodation:** Options range from budget guesthouses and hostels to mid-range hotels and luxury resorts. Beach fales, traditional open-sided huts, are a unique and affordable option for a more immersive experience.

- **Food:** Dining out can be inexpensive if you choose local eateries and markets. For a more upscale experience, several international restaurants in Apia and resort areas offer diverse cuisine. Self-catering is also an option, with supermarkets and local markets providing fresh produce and staples.

- **Activities:** Many of Samoa's natural attractions, such as beaches and waterfalls, are free or have a nominal entry fee. Guided tours, diving, and cultural experiences may have higher costs, so planning and budgeting for these activities in advance is recommended.

Tipping

Tipping is not a customary practice in Samoa. However, if you receive exceptional service, small gratuities are appreciated but not expected. Some higher-end restaurants and hotels may include a service charge in the bill.

Travel Insurance

Importance of Travel Insurance

Travel insurance is a crucial aspect of trip planning that can protect you from unexpected expenses and emergencies. A comprehensive travel insurance policy should cover various aspects, including medical emergencies, trip cancellations, lost luggage, and more.

Medical Coverage

Ensure your travel insurance includes adequate medical coverage. This should cover emergency medical treatment, hospital stays, and medical evacuation if necessary. Healthcare facilities in Samoa are generally limited, especially outside Apia, so having insurance that covers evacuation to a country with more advanced medical care is vital.

Trip Cancellation and Interruption

Unexpected events can disrupt travel plans, and insurance can provide peace of mind by covering costs related to trip cancellations or interruptions. Reasons for claims may include illness, natural disasters, or other unforeseen circumstances.

Lost or Delayed Baggage

Baggage delays or losses can be particularly frustrating. Insurance can help by reimbursing you for essential purchases and providing compensation for lost items. Keep receipts of any purchases made due to baggage delays to support your claim.

Adventure Activities

If you plan to engage in adventure activities like diving, surfing, or hiking, check that your insurance policy covers these activities. Some standard policies may exclude certain high-risk activities, so you might need to add specific coverage or choose a policy designed for adventure travelers.

Choosing a Policy

When selecting a travel insurance policy, consider the following:

- **Coverage Limits:** Ensure the policy limits are sufficient for your needs, especially for medical and evacuation coverage.

- **Exclusions:** Read the policy carefully to understand what is and isn't covered. Look out for exclusions related to pre-existing conditions, certain activities, or specific destinations.

- **Customer Reviews:** Research reviews and ratings of insurance providers to gauge their reliability and customer service.

- **Claims Process:** Choose a provider with a straightforward claims process and 24/7 customer support.

Documentation

Keep a copy of your insurance policy, including emergency contact numbers and your policy number, easily accessible during your trip. It's also wise to leave a copy with a friend or family member at home.

Planning your trip to Samoa involves considering various factors to ensure a safe and enjoyable experience. By understanding the best times to visit, fulfilling entry requirements, arranging transportation, managing your budget, and securing comprehensive travel insurance, you can embark on your Samoan adventure with confidence and excitement.

Samoa's natural beauty, rich culture, and friendly people make it a destination worth exploring. With thoughtful planning and preparation, your trip to Samoa in 2024 will be an unforgettable journey filled with discovery and joy. So pack your bags, prepare your itinerary, and get ready to experience the wonders of Samoa.

GETTING AROUND SAMOA

Exploring Samoa is a rewarding experience filled with stunning landscapes, vibrant culture, and warm hospitality. To make the most of your visit, understanding the various transportation options and safety considerations is essential. This guide covers public transportation, renting a car, exploring the islands, and safety tips for travelers.

Public Transportation Options

Buses

Samoan buses are a colorful and economical way to travel, offering a unique glimpse into local life. Buses in Samoa are often brightly painted and adorned with lively decorations, each with its own personality. They are a fun and cost-effective option for getting around, especially on the island of Upolu.

- **Routes and Schedules:** Buses in Samoa do not follow strict schedules, so patience and flexibility are required. They generally run from early morning until late afternoon. Major routes include Apia to various parts of Upolu, such as the southern coast and the eastern region. Each bus displays its destination on a signboard at the front, but asking the driver or locals for confirmation can be helpful.

- **Fares:** Bus fares are inexpensive, making them an attractive option for budget travelers. Payment is typically made in cash when boarding or exiting the bus. Having small denominations of Samoan Tala (WST) is recommended for convenience.

- **Experience:** Riding a Samoan bus is an adventure in itself. Expect to share the ride with locals, enjoy Samoan music playing, and possibly encounter a variety of goods being transported. While it may not be the fastest mode of transport, it offers a genuine cultural experience.

Taxis

Taxis are widely available and offer a convenient way to travel, especially for short distances or when public transport options are limited. They provide a more direct and comfortable means of getting around compared to buses.

- **Availability:** Taxis can be found throughout Apia and other major towns. They can be hailed on the street, booked through hotels, or found at taxi stands.

- **Fares:** Taxis in Samoa do not use meters, so it's essential to agree on the fare before starting your journey. Negotiating the price in advance helps avoid misunderstandings. Fares are generally reasonable, but it's wise to carry cash as credit cards are not commonly accepted.

- **Tips:** While tipping is not customary in Samoa, rounding up the fare as a gesture of appreciation for good service is always welcome.

Ferries

For inter-island travel, ferries are a vital mode of transportation, connecting the main islands of Upolu and Savai'i. The ferry service is reliable and offers an opportunity to enjoy scenic views of the surrounding ocean.

- **Routes and Schedules:** Ferries operate between Mulifanua Wharf on Upolu and Salelologa Wharf on Savai'i. The crossing takes about 90 minutes. Ferries run multiple times a day, but it's advisable to check the schedule in advance, as it can be affected by weather conditions.

- **Tickets:** Tickets can be purchased at the wharf or in advance through travel agencies and hotels. It's a good idea to arrive early, especially during peak travel times, to secure your spot.

- **Experience:** The ferry ride is generally smooth, providing a chance to relax and enjoy the journey. There are basic amenities on board, and you can often purchase snacks and drinks.

Renting a Car

Renting a car in Samoa offers the freedom and flexibility to explore at your own pace. It's an excellent option for travelers who prefer a more independent experience and wish to visit less accessible areas.

Rental Agencies

Car rental services are available in Apia, at Faleolo International Airport, and on Savai'i. Several international and local agencies operate in Samoa, providing a range of vehicles from compact cars to SUVs.

- **Requirements:** To rent a car in Samoa, you need a valid driver's license from your home country. Additionally, an international driving permit (IDP) is required, which can be obtained from the Ministry of Works, Transport, and Infrastructure in Apia. Most rental agencies also require a credit card for the security deposit.

- **Booking:** It's advisable to book your rental car in advance, especially during peak tourist seasons. Online reservations are available through agency websites, and many hotels can assist with bookings.

Driving in Samoa

Driving in Samoa is relatively straightforward, but it's important to be aware of local road conditions and regulations.

- **Road Conditions:** Major roads in Samoa are paved and in good condition, but secondary roads can be rough and may require a 4WD vehicle. Be prepared for narrow roads, occasional potholes, and livestock or pedestrians sharing the road.

- **Traffic Rules:** Samoans drive on the left side of the road. Speed limits are generally 40 km/h in urban areas and 55 km/h on open roads, though it's essential to adhere to posted signs. Seat belts are mandatory, and using a mobile phone while driving is prohibited.

- **Parking:** Parking is usually available at tourist sites, accommodations, and in Apia. However, finding parking in busy areas may require patience. Always park in designated areas and avoid blocking driveways or access points.

Fuel Stations

Fuel stations are available in Apia, along major routes, and in larger towns on Savai'i. It's a good idea to fill up the tank before embarking on long drives, especially when traveling to remote areas where fuel stations may be sparse.

Exploring the Islands

Samoa's two main islands, Upolu and Savai'i, each offer unique attractions and experiences. Exploring these islands requires a bit of planning to make the most of your visit.

Upolu

Upolu is the more developed of the two main islands, home to the capital city, Apia, and a variety of attractions.

- **Apia:** As the capital, Apia is the hub of activity with markets, shops, and cultural sites. Key attractions include the Robert Louis Stevenson Museum, the Samoa Cultural Village, and the bustling Maketi Fou (central market).

- **Beaches and Natural Sites:** Upolu boasts stunning beaches like Lalomanu and Lefaga, as well as natural wonders such as the To Sua Ocean Trench and the Papaseea Sliding Rocks. The island's interior is lush and green, with waterfalls like Papapapaitai Falls offering scenic beauty.

- **Cultural Experiences:** Visiting traditional villages provides insight into Samoan life and customs. Participating in a fiafia night, where you can enjoy traditional dance and music, is a highlight.

Savai'i

Savai'i, the larger but less developed island, offers a more laid-back and rural experience.

- **Natural Attractions:** Savai'i is known for its dramatic landscapes, including the Alofaaga Blowholes, the Saleaula Lava Fields, and the Afu Aau Waterfall. The island's rugged beauty and slower pace make it a great destination for nature lovers.

- **Cultural Sites:** Explore the village of Manase, known for its beach fales, or visit the Peapea Cave, home to swiftlets and unique geological formations.

- **Adventure Activities:** Savai'i offers opportunities for hiking, snorkeling, and diving. The coral reefs around the island are teeming with marine life, making it a fantastic spot for underwater exploration.

Safety Tips for Travelers

Ensuring your safety while traveling in Samoa involves being aware of your surroundings, following local customs, and taking basic precautions.

Health and Safety

- **Vaccinations:** While no specific vaccinations are required for entry, it's recommended to be up-to-date on routine vaccines. Depending on your travel history, a Yellow Fever vaccination certificate may be necessary.

- **Water Safety:** Tap water in Samoa is generally safe to drink in urban areas, but bottled water is recommended, especially in rural regions. Staying hydrated is important, particularly in the tropical climate.

- **Sun Protection:** The tropical sun can be intense, so using sunscreen, wearing hats, and staying in the shade during peak hours are essential to prevent sunburn and heatstroke.

Personal Safety

- **Respect Local Customs:** Samoans are known for their hospitality, but it's important to respect local customs and traditions. Dress modestly, especially in villages and during visits to cultural sites. Avoid public displays of affection, as they may be considered inappropriate.

- **Secure Belongings:** Petty theft can occur, so keep your belongings secure. Use hotel safes for valuables and avoid leaving items unattended on the beach or in public places.

- **Emergency Numbers:** Familiarize yourself with local emergency numbers. The general emergency number in Samoa is 911.

Natural Hazards

- **Weather Conditions:** Be aware of weather forecasts, especially during the wet season when heavy rains and cyclones can occur. Following local advice and taking necessary precautions during severe weather is crucial.

- **Swimming Safety:** Ocean currents and waves can be strong, so always swim in designated areas and heed any warnings from lifeguards or locals. Avoid swimming alone, and be cautious of sharp coral and marine life.

- **Driving Safety:** Drive cautiously, especially on unfamiliar or poorly maintained roads. Watch for pedestrians, animals, and other potential hazards. Use headlights at dusk and during rain for better visibility.

Environmental Responsibility

- **Conservation:** Samoa's natural beauty is one of its greatest assets. Help preserve it by following environmental guidelines, such as not littering, respecting wildlife, and sticking to marked trails.

- **Eco-Friendly Practices:** Participate in eco-friendly activities and support local businesses that prioritize sustainability. Simple actions like using reusable water bottles and bags can make a significant difference.

Getting around Samoa is part of the adventure, offering a chance to see the islands' diverse landscapes and experience the local way of life. Whether you choose the colorful buses, convenient taxis, or the independence of a rental car, each mode of transport provides its own unique perspective on this beautiful country.

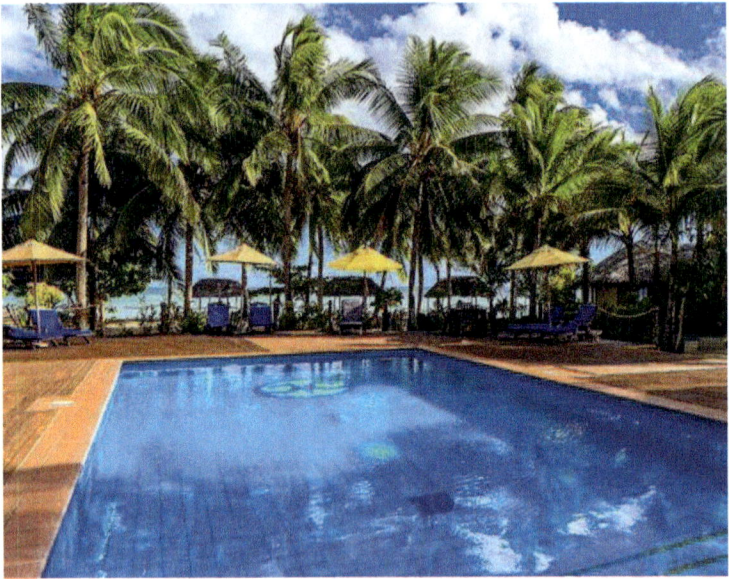

WHERE TO STAY

Samoa, a tropical paradise in the South Pacific, offers a range of accommodations to suit all travelers, from luxury resorts to budget-friendly options and unique stays. Whether you seek the comforts of a high-end hotel, the charm of a beach fale, or the eco-conscious appeal of an eco-lodge, Samoa has something for everyone. This guide will help you find the perfect place to stay during your visit.

Top Hotels and Resorts

Samoa is home to several top-notch hotels and resorts that provide luxurious accommodations and excellent amenities. These establishments often offer stunning views, private beaches, and top-tier services, making them ideal for those seeking a premium experience.

Taumeasina Island Resort

Located on a private island just off the coast of Apia, Taumeasina Island Resort offers a blend of modern luxury and Samoan hospitality. Guests can enjoy well-appointed rooms, villas with ocean views, and a variety of dining options. The resort features a spa, two swimming pools, and a range of water sports activities.

Sheraton Samoa Beach Resort

Situated on the island of Upolu, the Sheraton Samoa Beach Resort is a beachfront property that promises a relaxing stay. The resort boasts spacious rooms and suites with private balconies, an infinity pool, a fitness center, and multiple dining venues. The Sheraton is perfect for those looking to unwind in a serene environment.

Return to Paradise Resort

This resort, named after the famous 1953 movie filmed on its beach, offers a unique blend of historical charm and modern comfort. Located on the south coast of Upolu, Return to Paradise Resort features beachfront villas, a lagoon-style pool, and a range of activities such as snorkeling and cultural tours. The resort's restaurant serves delicious local and international cuisine.

Sinalei Reef Resort & Spa

For a more intimate and romantic experience, Sinalei Reef Resort & Spa is an excellent choice. This adults-only resort on Upolu's south coast offers luxurious fales and suites, a full-service spa, and a beautiful beachfront setting. Guests can enjoy activities such as kayaking, fishing, and traditional Samoan cooking classes.

Le Lagoto Resort & Spa

Located on the island of Savai'i, Le Lagoto Resort & Spa offers a tranquil retreat with stunning ocean views. The resort features beachfront bungalows, an infinity pool, and a restaurant serving fresh seafood and local dishes. It's an ideal spot for relaxation and exploring the natural beauty of Savai'i.

Budget Accommodations

Travelers on a budget will find plenty of affordable options in Samoa without sacrificing comfort or convenience. Budget accommodations range from guesthouses to motels and backpacker hostels, providing a cost-effective way to experience the islands.

Tatiana Motel

Tatiana Motel in Apia offers clean and comfortable rooms at budget-friendly prices. The motel provides basic amenities, including air conditioning, Wi-Fi, and a communal kitchen. Its central location makes it convenient for exploring the city's attractions, markets, and restaurants.

Taufua Beach Fales

For an authentic Samoan experience, Taufua Beach Fales on Lalomanu Beach offers traditional fale accommodations. These open-sided huts provide a rustic charm and direct access to one of Samoa's most beautiful beaches. Rates include breakfast and dinner, making it an excellent value for budget travelers.

Olivia's Accommodation

Located in Apia, Olivia's Accommodation offers simple yet cozy rooms with shared facilities. It's a great option for backpackers and budget-conscious travelers looking for a friendly and communal atmosphere. The guesthouse is within walking distance of local shops and eateries.

Faofao Beach Fales

Faofao Beach Fales, situated on the south coast of Upolu, offers budget-friendly beachside accommodations. The fales are basic but comfortable, and the property includes a restaurant serving local dishes. It's a great spot for those looking to enjoy the natural beauty of Samoa without spending much.

Unique Stays

For travelers seeking unique and eco-friendly accommodations, Samoa offers beach fales and eco-lodges that provide a closer connection to nature and local culture.

Beach Fales

Staying in a beach fale is a quintessential Samoan experience. These traditional open-sided huts are usually built on or near the beach, providing a rustic yet charming way to enjoy the island's natural beauty. Here are some notable beach fale accommodations:

- **Manase Beach Fales:** Located on Savai'i, Manase Beach Fales offers simple huts right on the beach. Guests can enjoy stunning sunsets, snorkeling, and the relaxed village atmosphere.

- **Litia Sini Beach Fales:** On the famous Lalomanu Beach, Litia Sini Beach Fales offers a blend of traditional fales and modern amenities. The property includes a restaurant and bar, and activities such as kayaking and hiking can be arranged.

Eco-Lodges

For those who prioritize sustainability and a deeper connection with nature, eco-lodges in Samoa provide an excellent option. These lodges focus on environmental conservation and community involvement while offering comfortable accommodations.

- **Seabreeze Resort:** Located on Upolu's south coast, Seabreeze Resort is an eco-friendly property that combines luxury with sustainability. The resort has adopted several green practices, including solar power and waste reduction. Guests can enjoy snorkeling, kayaking, and relaxing in well-appointed bungalows.

- **Coconuts Beach Club Resort & Spa:** This eco-lodge on Upolu's south coast offers beachfront fales and overwater bungalows. Coconuts Beach Club is committed to sustainable tourism practices, such as using local materials and supporting community projects. The resort features a spa, restaurant, and various water activities.

Neighborhood Guide

Understanding the different areas and neighborhoods in Samoa can help you choose the best place to stay based on your interests and activities. Here's a guide to some of the key areas:

Apia

As the capital city, Apia is the heart of Samoa's cultural and commercial activities. Staying in Apia offers easy access to markets, museums, restaurants, and nightlife. It's a great base for exploring the island of Upolu.

- **Attractions:** Robert Louis Stevenson Museum, Samoa Cultural Village, Maketi Fou (central market).

- **Accommodation Options:** A range of hotels, guesthouses, and motels to suit various budgets.

South Coast of Upolu

The south coast of Upolu is known for its stunning beaches, lush landscapes, and tranquil atmosphere. It's an ideal area for those seeking relaxation and natural beauty.

- **Attractions:** Lalomanu Beach, To Sua Ocean Trench, Papapapaitai Falls.

- **Accommodation Options:** Luxury resorts like Sinalei Reef Resort & Spa, beach fales such as Taufua Beach Fales.

North Coast of Upolu

The north coast offers a mix of beautiful beaches and cultural experiences. It's a quieter area compared to Apia, perfect for those looking to escape the hustle and bustle.

- **Attractions:** Piula Cave Pool, Falefa Falls, Le Mafa Pass.

- **Accommodation Options:** Mid-range hotels and guesthouses.

Savai'i

Savai'i is the larger but less developed island, offering a more laid-back and authentic Samoan experience. It's ideal for nature lovers and those interested in exploring traditional villages.

- **Attractions:** Alofaaga Blowholes, Saleaula Lava Fields, Afu Aau Waterfall.

- **Accommodation Options:** Le Lagoto Resort & Spa, beach fales in Manase, budget guesthouses.

Lalomanu

Lalomanu, located on the southeastern coast of Upolu, is famous for its picturesque beach and vibrant coral reefs. It's a popular spot for snorkeling, swimming, and enjoying the tranquil beach setting.

- **Attractions:** Lalomanu Beach, nearby waterfalls, traditional villages.

- **Accommodation Options:** Beach fales like Litia Sini Beach Fales, budget accommodations, and small resorts.

Choosing the right accommodation in Samoa depends on your preferences, budget, and the type of experience you seek. Whether you opt for the luxury of a top resort, the affordability of a budget guesthouse, or the unique charm of a beach fale or eco-lodge, Samoa's hospitality and natural beauty will make your stay memorable.

Each type of accommodation offers a different perspective on Samoan life, from the bustling streets of Apia to the serene beaches of the south coast and the rugged beauty of Savai'i. By understanding the options available, you can select the perfect place to rest and rejuvenate as you explore this stunning island paradise.

So pack your bags, set your itinerary, and get ready to experience the diverse and welcoming accommodations that Samoa has to offer. From luxury resorts to budget-friendly stays and unique eco-lodges, your perfect Samoan adventure awaits.

SAMOA'S MAIN ISLANDS

Samoa is an enchanting destination made up of two main islands, Upolu and Savai'i, each offering unique experiences and attractions. Upolu, known as the heart of Samoa, is where the capital city, Apia, is located and where most of the population resides. Savai'i, often referred to as the big island, is larger but less populated, offering a more rustic and natural experience. Exploring these islands provides a comprehensive view of Samoa's natural beauty, rich culture, and warm hospitality.

Upolu: The Heart of Samoa

Upolu is the most developed and populated island in Samoa. It is home to the capital city, Apia, and offers a vibrant mix of urban and natural attractions. From bustling markets to serene beaches, Upolu has something for everyone.

Apia: The Capital City

Apia is the beating heart of Samoa. This bustling city is where you will find the government, commercial centers, and cultural landmarks. Walking through Apia, you'll encounter a blend of traditional Samoan culture and modern influences.

- **Robert Louis Stevenson Museum:** This museum is the former home of the famous Scottish author who spent his final years in Samoa. The beautifully preserved house offers a glimpse into Stevenson's life and work. The surrounding gardens are perfect for a leisurely stroll, and the nearby Mount Vaea provides a rewarding hike with stunning views over Apia.

- **Samoa Cultural Village:** Located in the city center, the cultural village offers interactive experiences of Samoan traditions, including weaving, carving, and traditional cooking. It's a must-visit to understand the cultural richness of the Samoan people.

- **Maketi Fou:** This central market is a vibrant place to explore. Here, you can find fresh produce, handmade crafts, and local delicacies. It's an excellent spot to immerse yourself in the local way of life and pick up some unique souvenirs.

Coastal and Natural Attractions

Upolu boasts some of the most stunning natural attractions in Samoa. From pristine beaches to lush rainforests, the island's landscape is diverse and breathtaking.

- **Lalomanu Beach:** Often considered one of the best beaches in the South Pacific, Lalomanu Beach features powdery white sand and crystal-clear waters. It's a great spot for swimming, snorkeling, or simply relaxing under the sun.

- **To Sua Ocean Trench:** This natural swimming hole is a wonder to behold. Surrounded by lush gardens,

47

the To Sua Ocean Trench features a deep pool of clear blue water, accessible by a steep ladder. It's an iconic Samoan attraction and a fantastic spot for a refreshing dip.

- **Papapapaitai Falls:** One of the highest waterfalls in Samoa, Papapapaitai Falls cascades down over 100 meters into a deep gorge. The falls are surrounded by lush tropical vegetation, making it a picturesque spot for nature lovers.

Adventure and Activities

Upolu offers a variety of activities for those seeking adventure.

- **Hiking:** There are numerous hiking trails across Upolu, ranging from easy walks to challenging treks. One popular trail is the Mount Vaea hike, which leads to Robert Louis Stevenson's grave and offers panoramic views of Apia and the surrounding area.

- **Water Sports:** Upolu's coastal areas are perfect for water sports. Snorkeling, diving, and kayaking are popular activities, with many spots offering vibrant coral reefs and abundant marine life.

- **Surfing:** Samoa is known for its excellent surfing conditions, and Upolu has several great spots for surfers of all levels. The south coast, in particular, offers consistent waves and beautiful scenery.

Savai'i: The Big Island

Savai'i is the largest island in Samoa, known for its unspoiled landscapes and traditional villages. It offers a more tranquil and rustic experience compared to Upolu, making it perfect for those looking to escape the hustle and bustle and connect with nature.

Natural Attractions

Savai'i is a treasure trove of natural wonders, from volcanic landscapes to lush forests and pristine beaches.

- **Alofaaga Blowholes:** These spectacular blowholes on the south coast of Savai'i are a must-see. When waves crash into the lava tubes, water is forced through narrow openings, creating impressive geysers that shoot high into the air. It's a dramatic and mesmerizing natural phenomenon.

- **Saleaula Lava Fields:** The remnants of the 1905 volcanic eruption, the Saleaula Lava Fields offer a fascinating glimpse into Samoa's geological history. The lava flow buried several villages, and today, you can see the ruins, including a partially buried church, which stand as a testament to the power of nature.

- **Afu Aau Waterfall:** Located near the village of Vailoa, the Afu Aau Waterfall is a beautiful spot to visit. The waterfall cascades into a clear pool, perfect for swimming and cooling off. The surrounding area is lush and tranquil, offering a peaceful escape.

Cultural Experiences

Savai'i is known for its strong cultural traditions and vibrant village life. Visiting the island provides an opportunity to immerse yourself in Samoan culture.

- **Traditional Villages:** Many villages on Savai'i welcome visitors and offer insights into traditional Samoan life. You can participate in a traditional ava ceremony, learn about local crafts, and enjoy traditional feasts prepared in an umu (earth oven).

- **Falealupo Canopy Walkway:** This unique attraction offers a chance to explore the rainforest from above. The canopy walkway is a suspended bridge that takes you through the treetops, providing a different perspective on the island's flora and fauna.

Beaches and Marine Life

Savai'i boasts some of the most pristine and secluded beaches in Samoa, making it an ideal destination for beach lovers and marine enthusiasts.

- **Manase Beach:** This idyllic beach is located on the north coast of Savai'i. It's a perfect spot for swimming, snorkeling, and relaxing in a traditional beach fale. The waters are clear and calm, making it a great place for families.

- **Lano Beach:** Another beautiful beach on Savai'i, Lano Beach offers soft white sand and clear blue waters. It's less crowded than some of the more popular beaches, providing a peaceful and serene environment.

- **Diving and Snorkeling:** Savai'i offers excellent opportunities for diving and snorkeling. The coral reefs around the island are home to a diverse array of marine life, including colorful fish, sea turtles, and reef sharks. Several dive operators on the island offer guided tours and equipment rentals.

Travel Between the Islands

Traveling between Upolu and Savai'i is straightforward, with regular ferry services connecting the two islands. The ferry ride takes approximately 90 minutes and offers scenic views of the ocean and surrounding islands. It's advisable to book your ferry tickets in advance, especially during peak travel seasons.

Getting Around

Both Upolu and Savai'i have reliable transportation options, including rental cars, taxis, and public buses. Renting a car is a convenient way to explore the islands at your own pace. Public buses are an affordable option and offer a unique way to experience local life, though they may not adhere to strict schedules.

Accommodation

Accommodation options vary across the islands, from luxury resorts to budget-friendly beach fales and eco-lodges. In Upolu, you'll find a range of hotels in Apia and along the coast. Savai'i offers more rustic and traditional accommodations, providing an authentic Samoan experience.

Dining

Samoan cuisine is a highlight of any visit, featuring fresh seafood, tropical fruits, and traditional dishes. In Apia, you'll find a variety of restaurants and cafes offering local and international cuisine. On Savai'i, dining options are more limited but often include delicious meals prepared with locally sourced ingredients.

Exploring Samoa's main islands, Upolu and Savai'i, offers a diverse and enriching experience. Upolu, with its mix of urban and natural attractions, provides a vibrant and dynamic atmosphere. Savai'i, with its unspoiled landscapes and strong cultural traditions, offers a peaceful and authentic escape. Together, these islands showcase the best of Samoa's natural beauty, cultural richness, and warm hospitality.

Whether you're seeking adventure, relaxation, or cultural immersion, Samoa's main islands have something to offer every traveler. Plan your journey, explore the stunning landscapes, and create unforgettable memories in this tropical paradise.

MUST-SEE ATTRACTIONS

Samoa, an island nation in the South Pacific, is a treasure trove of natural beauty, rich history, and vibrant culture. Whether you're exploring the bustling streets of Apia, marveling at the natural wonders of the To Sua Ocean Trench, delving into literary history at the Robert Louis Stevenson Museum, relaxing on the pristine sands of Lalomanu Beach, or witnessing the raw power of nature at the Alofaaga Blowholes, Samoa offers an array of unforgettable experiences. This guide highlights some of the must-see attractions that should be on every visitor's itinerary.

Apia: Samoa's Capital City

Apia, the capital city of Samoa, is a vibrant hub of culture, history, and commerce. Situated on the island of Upolu, Apia is the gateway to exploring Samoa's many attractions. The city combines traditional Samoan charm with modern amenities, making it an ideal starting point for your Samoan adventure.

Cultural and Historical Sites

- **Samoa Cultural Village:** Located in the heart of Apia, the Samoa Cultural Village offers an immersive experience into Samoan traditions and way of life. Visitors can participate in traditional crafts like weaving and carving, witness a traditional ava (kava) ceremony, and enjoy cultural performances that showcase Samoan dance and music.

- **Mulivai Cathedral:** Also known as the Immaculate Conception of Mary Cathedral, this beautiful church is a landmark in Apia. The cathedral's stunning architecture and intricate stained glass windows are worth exploring, and it offers a peaceful retreat from the bustling city.

Markets and Shopping

- **Maketi Fou (Central Market):** A visit to Maketi Fou provides a colorful and lively experience. This central market is the place to find fresh produce, local handicrafts, traditional Samoan clothing, and unique souvenirs. The bustling atmosphere offers a glimpse into daily life in Apia.

- **Fugalei Market:** Another popular market in Apia, Fugalei Market specializes in fresh produce, seafood, and traditional Samoan foods. It's a great place to try local delicacies and interact with friendly vendors.

Dining and Nightlife

Apia boasts a variety of dining options, ranging from traditional Samoan fare to international cuisine. The city's nightlife includes bars, clubs, and live music venues where you can enjoy local talent and meet fellow travelers.

- **Paddles Restaurant:** Known for its excellent seafood and Italian-inspired dishes, Paddles offers a cozy dining experience with stunning views of the harbor.

- **Amanaki Restaurant:** Located within the Amanaki Hotel, this restaurant serves delicious Samoan and international cuisine. It's a popular spot for both locals and tourists.

To Sua Ocean Trench

One of Samoa's most iconic natural attractions, the To Sua Ocean Trench is a must-see for any visitor. This unique swimming hole is located in Lotofaga village on the south coast of Upolu. To Sua, which means "giant swimming hole," is a stunning example of Samoa's natural beauty.

The Experience

The To Sua Ocean Trench consists of a large, 30-meter deep hole filled with clear, turquoise water. It's accessible via a wooden ladder that descends from the edge of the trench to a platform near the water. Swimming in the trench is a surreal experience, surrounded by lush greenery and the sounds of nature.

Gardens and Surroundings

The area around To Sua Ocean Trench is beautifully landscaped with gardens, walking paths, and picnic areas.

There are also smaller trenches and blowholes nearby, adding to the natural allure of the site. It's an ideal place to spend a day relaxing, exploring, and enjoying the serene environment.

Practical Tips

- **Safety:** The ladder into the trench can be slippery, so take care when descending and climbing. It's advisable to wear water shoes for better grip.

- **Facilities:** There are changing rooms, restrooms, and picnic areas available for visitors. Bringing your own food and drinks is recommended, as there are no restaurants on-site.

Robert Louis Stevenson Museum

For literature enthusiasts and history buffs, the Robert Louis Stevenson Museum in Apia is a must-visit. This museum is dedicated to the famous Scottish author who spent the last years of his life in Samoa. Known locally as "Tusitala" (the teller of tales), Stevenson left a lasting legacy in Samoa, and his former home offers a fascinating insight into his life and work.

The Museum

Stevenson's beautifully preserved mansion, known as Vailima, is set in expansive gardens overlooking Apia. The museum's rooms are filled with personal artifacts, manuscripts, and photographs that tell the story of Stevenson's life and his connection to Samoa. Guided tours provide in-depth information about the author's literary achievements and his impact on Samoan culture.

Gardens and Grounds

The museum's gardens are a highlight in themselves, featuring lush tropical plants, manicured lawns, and pathways that lead to Stevenson's tomb on Mount Vaea. The hike to the tomb offers stunning views of Apia and the surrounding area, making it a rewarding activity for visitors.

Events and Activities

The museum hosts various events and activities throughout the year, including literary festivals, cultural performances, and educational programs. These events provide additional opportunities to learn about Stevenson's work and Samoan heritage.

Lalomanu Beach

Lalomanu Beach, located on the southeastern coast of Upolu, is often regarded as one of the most beautiful beaches in the South Pacific. With its powdery white sand, clear turquoise waters, and vibrant coral reefs, Lalomanu Beach is a paradise for beach lovers and water enthusiasts.

Beach Activities

- **Swimming and Snorkeling:** The calm, crystal-clear waters of Lalomanu Beach are perfect for swimming and snorkeling. The coral reefs close to shore are teeming with colorful marine life, making it an excellent spot for underwater exploration.

- **Sunbathing and Relaxation:** The soft, white sand provides an ideal setting for sunbathing and relaxation. Beach fales (traditional open-sided huts) are available for rent, offering shade and a unique experience of staying right on the beach.

- **Kayaking and Paddleboarding:** For those seeking a bit more activity, kayaking and paddleboarding are popular options. The gentle waves and stunning coastal scenery make for a delightful paddling experience.

Accommodation and Dining

Several accommodation options are available near Lalomanu Beach, ranging from budget-friendly beach fales to more upscale resorts. Staying overnight allows you to fully enjoy the beach's beauty and tranquility, especially during the early morning and late afternoon when the beach is less crowded.

- **Taufua Beach Fales:** One of the most popular places to stay, Taufua Beach Fales offers traditional fales right on the beach. The property includes a restaurant that serves delicious Samoan and international dishes, making it a convenient and enjoyable place to stay.

Practical Tips

- **Sun Protection:** The tropical sun can be intense, so be sure to bring plenty of sunscreen, hats, and sunglasses. Staying hydrated is also important, especially when spending extended time outdoors.

- **Respect for Local Culture:** While enjoying the beach, remember to respect local customs and traditions. Dress modestly when not swimming and be mindful of the environment by disposing of trash properly.

Alofaaga Blowholes

The Alofaaga Blowholes, located on the southwest coast of Savai'i, are a spectacular natural wonder. These blowholes are formed by lava tubes that connect the inland area with the ocean. When waves crash into the tubes, water is forced through the narrow openings, creating powerful geysers that shoot high into the air.

The Experience

Visiting the Alofaaga Blowholes is a thrilling experience. The force and height of the water jets depend on the tide and wave conditions, with the blowholes being most impressive during high tide and rough seas. The sight of water shooting up to 30 meters into the air is both awe-inspiring and humbling.

Safety Considerations

- **Distance:** It's important to keep a safe distance from the blowholes to avoid being caught by the powerful water jets. There are designated viewing areas that provide a good vantage point while ensuring safety.

- **Supervision:** If traveling with children, ensure they are closely supervised and kept away from the edges. The area around the blowholes can be slippery, so caution is advised.

Nearby Attractions

The region around the Alofaaga Blowholes offers additional attractions worth exploring. The nearby village of Taga is known for its traditional Samoan culture, and you can often find local guides who are happy to share stories and history about the area.

- **Saleaula Lava Fields:** A short drive from the blowholes, the Saleaula Lava Fields offer a fascinating glimpse into Samoa's volcanic history. The fields are the remnants of a volcanic eruption in 1905 that buried several villages. Today, you can see the ruins of a church and other structures that were partially engulfed by lava.

Samoa's must-see attractions offer a diverse array of experiences that highlight the natural beauty, cultural richness, and historical significance of this island nation. From the vibrant capital city of Apia to the breathtaking To Sua Ocean Trench, the literary heritage of the Robert Louis Stevenson Museum, the pristine sands of Lalomanu Beach, and the dramatic Alofaaga Blowholes, Samoa promises an unforgettable adventure for every visitor.

Whether you are a nature enthusiast, history buff, or simply looking to relax in a tropical paradise, Samoa's attractions cater to all interests and provide a unique glimpse into the heart

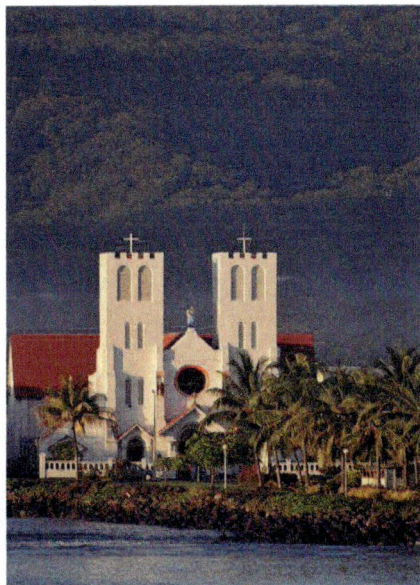

OUTDOOR ADVENTURES

Samoa, with its breathtaking landscapes, clear waters, and rich biodiversity, is a haven for outdoor enthusiasts. The islands offer a variety of activities that allow visitors to immerse themselves in nature and experience the beauty of this South Pacific paradise. From hiking trails and nature walks to snorkeling, diving, surfing, fishing, and wildlife watching, there's something for everyone. This guide provides an in-depth look at the outdoor adventures awaiting you in Samoa.

Hiking Trails and Nature Walks

Samoa's diverse terrain, from lush rainforests to volcanic landscapes, provides numerous opportunities for hiking and nature walks. Whether you're a seasoned hiker or prefer a leisurely stroll, Samoa has trails to suit all levels of fitness and interest.

Mount Vaea

Mount Vaea, overlooking Apia, is one of the most famous hikes in Samoa, primarily because it leads to the tomb of the beloved Scottish author Robert Louis Stevenson. The trail offers two routes: a shorter, steeper trail and a longer, more gradual path.

- **Short Trail:** This route is about 45 minutes to an hour each way and is steep but rewarding. As you ascend, you'll be treated to panoramic views of Apia and the surrounding area. At the summit, you'll find Stevenson's tomb, where you can take in the serene atmosphere and reflect on the author's legacy.

- **Long Trail:** The longer trail takes about an hour and a half each way and is less steep, making it suitable for those looking for a more leisurely hike. Both trails are well-maintained and clearly marked.

O Le Pupu-Puʿe National Park

Located on the south coast of Upolu, O Le Pupu-Puʿe National Park is Samoa's oldest national park, offering a range of hiking trails that wind through lush rainforest and along rugged coastline.

- **Togitogiga Waterfall Trail:** This short, easy trail leads to the beautiful Togitogiga Waterfall, where you can take a refreshing swim in the natural pools. The surrounding area is perfect for a picnic and offers plenty of opportunities to spot native birds and wildlife.

- **Coastal Walk:** For a more challenging hike, the park's coastal walk offers stunning views of the ocean and the chance to explore secluded beaches and rocky cliffs. The trail can be rugged in places, so sturdy footwear is recommended.

Lake Lanoto'o

Also known as Goldfish Lake, Lake Lanoto'o is a hidden gem located in the central highlands of Upolu. The trail to the lake is relatively short but can be muddy and slippery, especially after rain. Once you reach the lake, you'll be rewarded with tranquil waters surrounded by dense forest. The lake is home to goldfish, introduced by early settlers, which can often be seen swimming near the shore.

Snorkeling and Diving Spots

Samoa's clear, warm waters and vibrant coral reefs make it a prime destination for snorkeling and diving. The marine life is abundant and diverse, offering unforgettable underwater experiences.

Palolo Deep Marine Reserve

Just a short distance from Apia, Palolo Deep Marine Reserve is one of the best snorkeling spots in Samoa. The reserve features a deep blue hole surrounded by coral reefs teeming with marine life.

- **Snorkeling:** The calm, clear waters make for excellent visibility, allowing snorkelers to observe colorful fish, sea turtles, and vibrant corals. The reef is easily accessible from the shore, making it suitable for all levels of experience.

- **Diving:** For those interested in diving, the deeper parts of the reserve offer the chance to see larger marine species and explore underwater caves and crevices.

Alofaaga Caves

Located on the island of Savai'i, the Alofaaga Caves are another excellent spot for snorkeling and diving. The caves feature a series of underwater chambers filled with fascinating rock formations and a diverse array of marine life.

- **Snorkeling:** The shallow areas around the caves are perfect for snorkeling, with plenty of fish and corals to observe. The water is clear and calm, providing excellent conditions for exploring.

- **Diving:** Experienced divers can explore the deeper parts of the caves, which require careful navigation but offer stunning sights and a sense of adventure.

Lalomanu Beach

Lalomanu Beach, located on the southeastern coast of Upolu, is renowned for its stunning beauty and excellent snorkeling opportunities. The calm, crystal-clear waters are ideal for observing the vibrant coral reefs and the diverse marine life they support.

- **Snorkeling:** The reefs at Lalomanu Beach are easily accessible from the shore, making it a popular spot for families and beginner snorkelers. You'll encounter a variety of tropical fish, sea turtles, and other marine creatures.

Surfing in Samoa

Samoa is a world-class surfing destination, with consistent waves and beautiful surroundings. The islands offer a variety of breaks suitable for all levels, from beginners to experienced surfers.

Upolu's South Coast

The south coast of Upolu is known for its excellent surfing conditions, with consistent swells and a range of breaks.

- **Boulders:** This powerful reef break is best suited for experienced surfers. The waves are fast and hollow, providing thrilling rides but also requiring a high level of skill and confidence.

- **Salani:** A more forgiving break, Salani offers both left and right-hand waves that are suitable for intermediate to advanced surfers. The surrounding area is beautiful, with lush vegetation and stunning views of the coastline.

Savai'i's North Coast

Savai'i's north coast also boasts some great surfing spots, with less crowded waves and a more laid-back atmosphere.

- **Aganoa:** This consistent reef break offers both left and right-hand waves, suitable for intermediate to advanced surfers. The break is located near a surf camp, providing convenient access and a friendly community of surfers.

- **Mata'utu:** A less well-known spot, Mata'utu offers uncrowded waves and beautiful surroundings. The break is best suited for experienced surfers due to the powerful and sometimes unpredictable waves.

Surf Schools and Camps

For those new to surfing or looking to improve their skills, Samoa has several surf schools and camps that offer lessons and guided trips. These schools provide all the necessary equipment and instruction, making it easy to get started and enjoy the waves safely.

Fishing and Boat Tours

The waters around Samoa are rich with marine life, making it a fantastic destination for fishing and boat tours. Whether you're an experienced angler or just looking for a relaxing day on the water, there are plenty of options to choose from.

Deep-Sea Fishing

Samoa's deep-sea fishing is world-renowned, with opportunities to catch big game fish such as marlin, tuna, and mahi-mahi. Several charter companies offer guided fishing trips, providing all the necessary equipment and local expertise.

- **Charter Companies:** Charter companies such as Samoa Fishing Adventures and Troppo Fishing offer half-day and full-day trips, with experienced guides who know the best fishing spots. These trips often include refreshments and all the gear needed for a successful day on the water.

- **Fishing Tournaments:** Samoa hosts several fishing tournaments throughout the year, attracting anglers from around the world. These events offer the chance to compete, socialize, and enjoy the camaraderie of the fishing community.

Boat Tours

For those who prefer a more relaxed experience, boat tours are a great way to explore the coastline and nearby islands. These tours offer opportunities for sightseeing, snorkeling, and wildlife watching.

- **Coastal Cruises:** Coastal cruises around Upolu and Savai'i provide stunning views of the islands' landscapes, from dramatic cliffs to pristine beaches.

Many tours include stops for snorkeling and swimming, allowing you to explore the underwater world as well.

- **Island Hopping:** Island hopping tours take you to some of Samoa's smaller, less-visited islands. These tours often include opportunities to visit traditional villages, relax on secluded beaches, and enjoy picnics in picturesque settings.

Wildlife and Bird Watching

Samoa's diverse ecosystems support a wide variety of wildlife, making it an excellent destination for bird watchers and nature enthusiasts. The islands' forests, wetlands, and coastal areas are home to many unique and endemic species.

Samoa's Endemic Birds

Samoa is home to several endemic bird species, making it a prime destination for bird watchers.

- **Samoan Whistler:** This small, colorful bird is found only in Samoa and is known for its distinctive song. It inhabits forested areas on both Upolu and Savai'i.

- **Samoan Moorhen:** Also known as the Samoan Woodhen, this rare and elusive bird is critically endangered and can be found in the upland forests of

Savai'i. Efforts are ongoing to protect its habitat and increase its population.

- **Samoan Triller:** Another endemic species, the Samoan Triller can be seen flitting through the forest canopy, often in pairs or small groups.

Wildlife Sanctuaries and Conservation Areas

Several wildlife sanctuaries and conservation areas in Samoa provide excellent opportunities for observing native wildlife and learning about conservation efforts.

- **Vaoto Marine Reserve:** Located on the island of Manono, this marine reserve is a haven for birdlife and marine species. It's an excellent spot for bird watching, snorkeling, and learning about local conservation initiatives.

- **Apolima Island:** This small, remote island is home to a variety of bird species and offers a peaceful retreat for nature lovers. The island's unspoiled environment provides a glimpse into Samoa's natural beauty and biodiversity.

Guided Tours and Ecotourism

For those looking to enhance their wildlife and bird watching experience, guided tours and ecotourism activities are available. Knowledgeable guides can provide insights into the local flora and fauna, helping you spot and identify different species.

- **Bird Watching Tours:** Several tour operators offer bird watching tours that take you to prime birding locations on Upolu and Savai'i. These tours often include transportation, binoculars, and expert guides who can help you make the most of your birding experience.

- **Ecotourism Activities:** Ecotourism activities, such as guided hikes and educational programs, provide opportunities to learn about Samoa's ecosystems and conservation efforts. These activities are designed to be both informative and enjoyable, promoting sustainable tourism and environmental stewardship.

Samoa is a paradise for outdoor enthusiasts, offering a wide range of activities that allow you to immerse yourself in the natural beauty and rich biodiversity of the islands. From hiking through lush rainforests and exploring underwater worlds to riding the waves and observing unique wildlife, there's no shortage of adventures to be had.

By participating in these outdoor activities, you'll not only create unforgettable memories but also gain a deeper appreciation for Samoa's natural heritage and cultural traditions. Whether you're a thrill-seeker or simply looking to relax and enjoy the scenery, Samoa's outdoor adventures offer something for everyone.

So pack your gear, lace up your hiking boots, and get ready to experience the best of Samoa's great outdoors. With its stunning landscapes, diverse wildlife, and warm hospitality, Samoa is sure to leave you with a sense of wonder and a desire to return for more adventures.

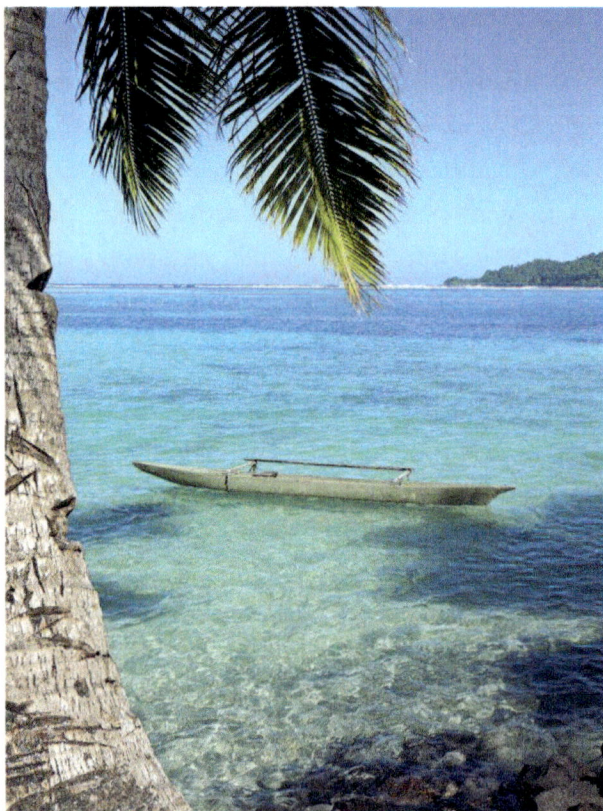

CULTURAL EXPERIENCES

Samoa, a gem in the South Pacific, is renowned for its vibrant culture and rich traditions. The cultural experiences here are deeply rooted in the customs and practices that have been passed down through generations. From exploring traditional Samoan villages and participating in local festivals to savoring the unique cuisine and appreciating the arts and crafts, Samoa offers a wealth of cultural encounters that provide a deep understanding of this beautiful island nation.

Traditional Samoan Villages

Visiting traditional Samoan villages is a highlight for many travelers, offering an authentic glimpse into the everyday life and customs of the Samoan people. The village is the heart of Samoan society, where community, family, and culture come together in a harmonious blend.

Village Structure and Life

Samoan villages are typically composed of a collection of fale (traditional thatched houses) arranged around a central open area known as the malae. The malae is the communal space where meetings, ceremonies, and social gatherings take place. Each village is led by a matai (chief), who plays a crucial role in maintaining order and overseeing communal activities.

- **Fa'a Samoa (The Samoan Way):** Fa'a Samoa, or the Samoan way of life, emphasizes respect, family, and community. Visitors to traditional villages can observe and participate in daily activities that reflect these values, such as communal cooking, weaving, and fishing.

- **Traditional Ceremonies:** Witnessing traditional ceremonies, such as the ava (kava) ceremony, provides a deep insight into Samoan customs. The ava ceremony is a formal ritual involving the preparation and drinking of ava, a ceremonial beverage made from the roots of the kava plant. This ceremony is an essential aspect of Samoan hospitality and social life.

Cultural Tours and Homestays

Many villages welcome visitors through organized cultural tours and homestays, providing an immersive experience.

- **Cultural Tours:** Guided cultural tours often include visits to significant sites within the village, demonstrations of traditional crafts and skills, and explanations of local customs and history. These tours offer a respectful and informative way to engage with the local culture.

- **Homestays:** Staying with a Samoan family allows for a deeper connection with the community. Homestays provide a unique opportunity to experience daily life firsthand, share meals, and learn about traditions and practices in an intimate setting.

Local Festivals and Events

Samoa's vibrant festivals and events are a testament to the island's rich cultural heritage and communal spirit. These celebrations are colorful, energetic, and filled with traditional music, dance, and food.

Teuila Festival

One of the largest and most famous festivals in Samoa, the Teuila Festival is held annually in the first week of September. Named after Samoa's national flower, the Teuila, this festival showcases the best of Samoan culture.

- **Cultural Performances:** The Teuila Festival features spectacular cultural performances, including traditional dances such as the siva and the fire knife dance. These performances are a visual and auditory feast, highlighting the skill and artistry of Samoan dancers and musicians.

- **Arts and Crafts Exhibitions:** The festival includes exhibitions of Samoan arts and crafts, where visitors can see and purchase items such as siapo (tapa cloth), wood carvings, and fine mats. Artisans often demonstrate their techniques, providing insight into the craftsmanship involved.

- **Traditional Sports:** Traditional Samoan sports, such as fautasi (longboat) racing and tug-of-war, are integral parts of the festival. These events are exciting to watch and reflect the communal and competitive spirit of Samoan society.

Independence Day

Samoa's Independence Day, celebrated on June 1st, marks the nation's independence from New Zealand in 1962. The day is filled with patriotic pride and festivities.

- **Parades and Ceremonies:** The celebrations in Apia, the capital, include a grand parade featuring schoolchildren, military personnel, and cultural groups. Official ceremonies honor the nation's history and achievements, with speeches and performances.

- **Feasts and Celebrations:** Villages and communities across Samoa hold feasts and celebrations, featuring traditional foods, music, and dance. It's a day of national pride and communal joy, where locals and visitors alike can join in the festivities.

Other Cultural Events

Throughout the year, various other cultural events take place in Samoa, each offering a unique glimpse into the island's traditions.

- **Fire Knife Dance Competitions:** These competitions are held at different times and locations, showcasing the incredible skill and bravery of Samoan fire knife dancers. The performances are thrilling and highlight an important aspect of Samoan culture.

- **Church Choir Competitions:** Samoan choirs are renowned for their harmonious singing. Choir competitions, often held during church festivals and special occasions, are a testament to the musical talent and spiritual devotion of the Samoan people.

Samoan Cuisine and Dining

Samoan cuisine is a delightful blend of traditional ingredients and cooking methods, reflecting the island's agricultural abundance and cultural heritage. Dining in Samoa offers a chance to savor unique flavors and enjoy the communal experience of sharing food.

Traditional Foods

Samoan cuisine is characterized by its use of fresh, locally sourced ingredients, including root vegetables, tropical fruits, seafood, and pork.

- **Umu (Earth Oven):** The umu is a traditional method of cooking where food is wrapped in leaves and cooked over hot stones. This method imparts a distinctive smoky flavor to dishes. Typical umu-cooked foods include taro, breadfruit, fish, and pork.

- **Palusami:** Palusami is a popular dish made from taro leaves filled with coconut cream and sometimes mixed with onions and meat. The leaves are folded into parcels and baked, resulting in a rich and flavorful dish.

- **Oka:** Oka is a refreshing raw fish salad, similar to ceviche. Fresh fish is marinated in lemon juice and mixed with coconut cream, onions, and vegetables. It's a perfect dish for warm tropical days.

Dining Experiences

Samoan dining is not just about the food; it's about the communal experience and the hospitality that accompanies it.

- **Fiafia Nights:** Many hotels and resorts in Samoa offer fiafia nights, which are traditional feasts accompanied by cultural performances. Guests can enjoy a buffet of

Samoan dishes while watching traditional dances and fire knife performances.

- **Village Feasts:** Participating in a village feast is a memorable experience. These feasts are often held to celebrate special occasions and involve a wide array of traditional foods prepared by the community. Guests are welcomed warmly and treated to the best of Samoan hospitality.

Local Markets and Street Food

Exploring local markets and street food stalls is a great way to experience the flavors of Samoa.

- **Apia's Maketi Fou:** This central market is a bustling hub where you can find fresh produce, cooked foods, and traditional Samoan delicacies. It's an excellent place to try dishes like BBQ chicken, grilled fish, and fresh tropical fruits.

- **Street Food Stalls:** Throughout Apia and other towns, street food stalls offer quick and tasty meals, such as taro chips, banana fritters, and coconut buns. These stalls provide a convenient and affordable way to sample local cuisine.

Arts and Crafts

Samoan arts and crafts are an integral part of the island's cultural heritage, reflecting the skills and creativity of the Samoan people. From intricate weaving and carving to the vibrant art of siapo making, these crafts are both beautiful and functional.

Siapo (Tapa Cloth)

Siapo, or tapa cloth, is one of Samoa's most renowned traditional crafts. Made from the bark of the paper mulberry tree, siapo is decorated with intricate designs using natural dyes.

- **Process:** The process of making siapo is labor-intensive and involves stripping the bark, soaking it, and beating it into a fine cloth. The cloth is then decorated with patterns that often depict local flora, fauna, and cultural symbols.

- **Uses:** Siapo is used for various purposes, including clothing, ceremonial items, and wall hangings. It is highly valued and often presented as a gift during important occasions.

Weaving

Weaving is a highly developed craft in Samoa, with skills passed down through generations. The most common items produced are mats, baskets, and fans.

- **Fine Mats:** Fine mats, known as ie toga, are especially significant in Samoan culture. They are used in ceremonies and given as gifts to mark important life events. The mats are woven from pandanus leaves and can take months or even years to complete.

- **Baskets and Fans:** Baskets and fans are everyday items that showcase the artistry of Samoan weaving. They are often sold at markets and make for practical and beautiful souvenirs.

Wood Carving

Wood carving is another traditional Samoan craft, with artisans creating a variety of items ranging from ceremonial objects to everyday tools.

- **Kava Bowls:** Kava bowls, or tanoa, are used in the traditional ava ceremony. These bowls are intricately carved from wood and are an important symbol of Samoan hospitality and culture.

- **War Clubs and Walking Sticks:** Historically, war clubs were used in battle, but today they are crafted as decorative items. Walking sticks, often carved with detailed designs, are also popular and showcase the carvers' skill.

Contemporary Arts

In addition to traditional crafts, Samoa has a growing contemporary arts scene. Local artists are increasingly blending traditional motifs with modern techniques, creating works that reflect both their heritage and contemporary influences.

- **Painting and Sculpture:** Samoan painters and sculptors are gaining recognition for their work, which often incorporates themes of identity, community, and the natural environment.

- **Performing Arts:** Dance and music remain vital components of Samoan culture, with traditional performances being a central feature of many events and celebrations. Contemporary dance groups and musicians are also emerging, adding new dimensions to Samoa's artistic landscape.

Cultural experiences in Samoa offer a deep and enriching understanding of this island nation's heritage and traditions. From the warmth and hospitality of traditional villages to the vibrant celebrations of local festivals, the unique flavors of Samoan cuisine, and the artistry of Samoan crafts, each experience provides a window into the soul of Samoa.

By engaging with these cultural elements, visitors can appreciate the values that underpin Samoan society and the ways in which tradition and modernity coexist harmoniously. Whether you are participating in a village ceremony, enjoying a fiafia night, browsing through local markets, or admiring the craftsmanship of a fine mat, you will leave with a greater appreciation for the depth and beauty of Samoan culture.

So immerse yourself in the rich tapestry of experiences that Samoa offers, and let the island's culture and people leave a lasting impression on your heart and mind.

RELAXATION AND WELLNESS

Samoa, with its serene beaches, luxurious spas, tranquil yoga retreats, and rejuvenating hot springs, offers the perfect setting for relaxation and wellness. Whether you seek to unwind by the ocean, pamper yourself with spa treatments, find inner peace through yoga and meditation, or soak in the natural hot springs, Samoa provides a holistic approach to well-being. This guide explores the best spots for relaxation and wellness across the islands.

Best Beaches for Relaxation

Samoa's beaches are renowned for their pristine beauty, offering ideal spots for relaxation and rejuvenation. The calm waters, soft sands, and stunning scenery make these beaches perfect for unwinding and escaping the hustle and bustle of everyday life.

Lalomanu Beach

Lalomanu Beach, located on the southeastern coast of Upolu, is often cited as one of the most beautiful beaches in the South Pacific. Its powdery white sand and clear turquoise waters create a picturesque setting for relaxation.

- **Tranquil Setting:** The serene atmosphere of Lalomanu Beach is perfect for sunbathing, reading a book, or simply enjoying the sound of the waves. The beach is relatively quiet, allowing for a peaceful retreat.

- **Beach Fales:** Traditional beach fales (open-sided huts) are available for rent along the shore, providing shade and a comfortable spot to relax. These fales offer an authentic Samoan experience and a chance to stay right on the beach.

Matareva Beach

Matareva Beach, on the southern coast of Upolu, is a hidden gem known for its secluded and tranquil environment. The beach is surrounded by lush vegetation and features soft sand and clear waters.

- **Seclusion:** Matareva Beach is less crowded than some of the more popular beaches, making it an ideal spot for those seeking solitude and relaxation. The peaceful ambiance is perfect for unwinding.

- **Snorkeling:** The calm waters of Matareva Beach are excellent for snorkeling. You can explore the vibrant coral reefs and observe the diverse marine life while enjoying the tranquility of the beach.

Aganoa Beach

Located on the southern coast of Savai'i, Aganoa Beach offers a stunning natural setting with its pristine sands and clear waters. The beach is a haven for relaxation and offers a sense of isolation from the outside world.

- **Natural Beauty:** Aganoa Beach is surrounded by lush greenery and features crystal-clear waters, making it a perfect spot for swimming and lounging. The unspoiled natural beauty adds to the beach's appeal.

- **Surfing:** For those who enjoy surfing, Aganoa Beach is known for its consistent waves. Surfing here can be both exhilarating and relaxing, as you ride the waves and connect with the ocean.

Spas and Wellness Retreats

Samoa's spas and wellness retreats offer a range of treatments and therapies designed to rejuvenate the body and mind. These establishments combine traditional Samoan healing practices with modern wellness techniques, providing a holistic approach to relaxation.

Sinalei Reef Resort & Spa

Sinalei Reef Resort & Spa, located on the south coast of Upolu, is an adults-only resort that offers a luxurious spa experience. The resort's spa is set in a tranquil garden, providing a serene environment for relaxation.

- **Signature Treatments:** The spa offers a variety of treatments, including traditional Samoan massage, hot stone therapy, and body wraps. These treatments use natural ingredients and techniques to promote relaxation and healing.

- **Wellness Packages:** Sinalei Reef Resort & Spa offers wellness packages that combine spa treatments with activities such as yoga, meditation, and healthy dining options. These packages are designed to provide a comprehensive wellness experience.

Le Lagoto Resort & Spa

Le Lagoto Resort & Spa, situated on the north coast of Savai'i, provides a peaceful and rejuvenating spa experience. The spa's location, overlooking the ocean, adds to the sense of tranquility.

- **Ocean-View Treatments:** Guests can enjoy massages and other treatments while listening to the sound of the waves. The ocean view enhances the relaxation experience and provides a soothing backdrop.

- **Traditional Techniques:** The spa incorporates traditional Samoan healing techniques, such as the use of local oils and herbs, into its treatments. These methods are aimed at restoring balance and promoting well-being.

Return to Paradise Resort & Spa

Return to Paradise Resort & Spa, on the south coast of Upolu, offers a range of spa services in a luxurious setting.

The resort's spa is designed to provide a sanctuary of relaxation and rejuvenation.

- **Holistic Treatments:** The spa offers holistic treatments that include massages, facials, and body scrubs. The use of natural products and personalized care ensures a rejuvenating experience.

- **Spa Packages:** Guests can choose from a variety of spa packages that combine different treatments for a comprehensive wellness experience. These packages are perfect for those looking to indulge in a day of pampering.

Yoga and Meditation Spots

Samoa's serene environment makes it an ideal destination for yoga and meditation. The natural beauty and peaceful atmosphere provide the perfect backdrop for finding inner peace and enhancing well-being.

Samoa Yoga Retreat

Samoa Yoga Retreat, located on the south coast of Upolu, offers a serene setting for yoga and meditation. The retreat provides a holistic approach to wellness, focusing on the mind, body, and spirit.

- **Daily Yoga Classes:** The retreat offers daily yoga classes that cater to all levels, from beginners to advanced practitioners. The classes are held in a tranquil outdoor setting, allowing participants to connect with nature.

- **Meditation Sessions:** Guided meditation sessions are also available, helping participants to find inner peace and reduce stress. The serene environment enhances the meditation experience, providing a sense of calm and tranquility.

Saletoga Sands Resort & Spa

Saletoga Sands Resort & Spa, located on the southeast coast of Upolu, offers yoga and meditation sessions in a beautiful beachfront setting. The resort's wellness programs are designed to promote relaxation and well-being.

- **Beachfront Yoga:** Guests can participate in yoga classes held on the beach, allowing them to practice with the sound of the waves and the gentle sea breeze. The classes are suitable for all levels and focus on relaxation and mindfulness.

- **Private Sessions:** Private yoga and meditation sessions are also available, providing a personalized experience. These sessions can be tailored to individual needs and preferences, ensuring a truly relaxing experience.

Coconuts Beach Club Resort & Spa

Coconuts Beach Club Resort & Spa, situated on the south coast of Upolu, offers yoga and wellness programs in a tranquil setting. The resort's focus on holistic wellness makes it an ideal destination for those seeking relaxation and rejuvenation.

- **Yoga and Wellness Retreats:** The resort offers yoga and wellness retreats that combine yoga practice with spa treatments and healthy dining. These retreats provide a comprehensive approach to well-being, allowing guests to relax and recharge.

- **Outdoor Yoga:** Yoga classes are held in outdoor pavilions with views of the ocean or gardens. The natural surroundings enhance the yoga practice and provide a sense of peace and tranquility.

Natural Hot Springs

Samoa's natural hot springs offer a unique and rejuvenating experience. The mineral-rich waters are known for their therapeutic properties, providing relaxation and relief from aches and pains.

Savai'i's Afu Aau Waterfall and Hot Springs

The Afu Aau Waterfall on the island of Savai'i is a popular destination for its stunning natural beauty and soothing hot springs.

- **Therapeutic Waters:** The hot springs at Afu Aau are rich in minerals and are believed to have healing properties. Soaking in the warm waters can help to relax muscles, improve circulation, and relieve stress.

- **Scenic Surroundings:** The hot springs are located near the waterfall, providing a picturesque setting. The combination of the warm waters and the sound of the waterfall creates a peaceful and rejuvenating atmosphere.

Pulemelei Hot Springs

The Pulemelei Hot Springs, also located on Savai'i, offer a unique experience in a serene environment. These natural springs are lesser-known, providing a tranquil and private setting for relaxation.

- **Remote Location:** The hot springs are situated in a remote area, away from the crowds. This seclusion adds to the sense of peace and allows for a truly relaxing experience.

- **Healing Properties:** The mineral-rich waters of the Pulemelei Hot Springs are said to have therapeutic benefits. Soaking in the springs can help to alleviate muscle pain, reduce inflammation, and promote overall well-being.

Papaseea Sliding Rocks

While not a hot spring, the Papaseea Sliding Rocks on Upolu offer a refreshing and fun water experience. These natural rock slides are fed by cool spring water and provide a unique way to enjoy the natural beauty of Samoa.

- **Natural Slides:** The smooth rocks create natural slides that lead into cool pools of water. It's a fun and invigorating activity that's perfect for cooling off on a warm day.

- **Scenic Beauty:** The sliding rocks are surrounded by lush tropical vegetation, making it a beautiful spot to relax and enjoy the natural surroundings.

Samoa's relaxation and wellness offerings are as diverse as its landscapes, providing a holistic approach to rejuvenation and well-being. From the pristine beaches and luxurious spas to the tranquil yoga retreats and therapeutic hot springs, there are countless ways to unwind and restore your mind, body, and spirit.

Whether you are seeking solitude on a secluded beach, indulging in a pampering spa treatment, finding inner peace through yoga and meditation, or soaking in the healing waters of natural hot springs, Samoa offers a sanctuary for relaxation and wellness. Embrace the serene environment, connect with nature, and let the beauty and tranquility of Samoa nourish your soul.

DAY TRIPS AND EXCURSIONS

Samoa, with its stunning landscapes and rich cultural heritage, offers a wealth of day trips and excursions for travelers seeking adventure and exploration. From the bustling capital city of Apia to the tranquil islands of Manono and Apolima, and the awe-inspiring waterfalls scattered throughout the islands, Samoa provides countless opportunities for unforgettable experiences. This guide delves into the top day trips from Apia, explores the hidden gems of Manono and Apolima, and highlights the best waterfall adventures.

Top Day Trips from Apia

Apia, the vibrant capital of Samoa, serves as a perfect base for numerous day trips that showcase the island's natural beauty and cultural richness. Here are some of the top excursions that can be enjoyed within a day from Apia.

1. To Sua Ocean Trench

Located on the south coast of Upolu, To Sua Ocean Trench is one of Samoa's most iconic natural attractions. This giant swimming hole, surrounded by lush gardens, offers a unique and picturesque setting for a day trip.

- **Swimming Experience:** The crystal-clear waters of To Sua are perfect for a refreshing swim. A wooden ladder leads down into the trench, making it accessible for swimmers of all levels. The serene environment and striking natural beauty create a memorable experience.

- **Picnic Spots:** The surrounding gardens are ideal for picnics. There are several sheltered areas with tables and benches where visitors can relax and enjoy a meal amidst the beautiful scenery.

2. Robert Louis Stevenson Museum

Just a short drive from Apia, the Robert Louis Stevenson Museum offers a fascinating insight into the life of the famous author who spent his final years in Samoa. The museum is set in Stevenson's former home, a beautiful colonial mansion known as Vailima.

- **Guided Tours:** The museum offers guided tours that provide detailed information about Stevenson's life and work. The rooms are filled with personal artifacts, photographs, and manuscripts that tell the story of his time in Samoa.

- **Gardens and Hiking:** The surrounding gardens are lush and well-maintained, providing a peaceful setting for a leisurely stroll. For those seeking a bit more activity, a hike up Mount Vaea to Stevenson's tomb offers stunning views of Apia and the surrounding area.

3. Piula Cave Pool

Located on the north coast of Upolu, Piula Cave Pool is a natural freshwater pool situated next to the historic Piula Theological College. This idyllic spot is perfect for a relaxing day trip.

- **Swimming and Snorkeling:** The clear, cool waters of Piula Cave Pool are perfect for swimming and snorkeling. The pool is fed by an underground spring and is surrounded by a cave, adding to its unique charm.

- **Picnicking:** The grassy areas around the pool are great for picnicking. Visitors can bring their own food or purchase snacks from nearby vendors and enjoy a relaxing day by the water.

4. Palolo Deep Marine Reserve

For those interested in marine life, Palolo Deep Marine Reserve is a must-visit. Located just a short walk from Apia, this underwater reserve offers excellent snorkeling and diving opportunities.

- **Snorkeling:** The reserve features a deep blue hole surrounded by vibrant coral reefs teeming with marine life. Snorkelers can observe a variety of colorful fish, sea turtles, and other marine creatures in the clear waters.

- **Diving:** For more experienced divers, the deeper parts of the reserve offer a chance to explore underwater caves and observe larger marine species. The visibility is excellent, making it a great spot for underwater photography.

Exploring the Islands of Manono and Apolima

The islands of Manono and Apolima, located off the western coast of Upolu, offer a tranquil escape from the hustle and bustle of the main islands. These smaller islands provide a glimpse into traditional Samoan life and are perfect for a day of exploration and relaxation.

1. Manono Island

Manono Island is known for its traditional way of life, beautiful landscapes, and friendly inhabitants. A visit to this island offers a peaceful and culturally enriching experience.

- **Cultural Immersion:** Manono Island is free of cars, providing a tranquil environment. Visitors can explore the island on foot, visiting traditional villages and experiencing the Samoan way of life. The locals are welcoming and often happy to share their customs and stories.

- **Scenic Walks:** The island offers several scenic walking trails that lead through lush vegetation and along the coastline. A walk around the island takes about three to four hours and provides stunning views of the surrounding ocean and neighboring islands.

- **Historical Sites:** Manono Island is home to several historical sites, including ancient star mounds and old church ruins. These sites offer a glimpse into the island's rich history and cultural heritage.

2. Apolima Island

Apolima Island, the smallest of Samoa's inhabited islands, is a hidden gem with a unique charm. The island is home to a small village and offers a quiet retreat for visitors.

- **Village Life:** The single village on Apolima Island is home to a close-knit community. Visitors can experience the simplicity and beauty of traditional Samoan life, with opportunities to participate in daily activities and learn about local customs.

- **Natural Beauty:** Apolima Island features rugged landscapes, pristine beaches, and clear waters. The island's natural beauty is perfect for photography, swimming, and snorkeling.

- **Boat Tours:** Access to Apolima Island is by boat, typically from the nearby island of Manono. Boat tours offer a scenic journey and the chance to see marine life such as dolphins and sea turtles.

Waterfall Adventures

Samoa's lush interior is dotted with stunning waterfalls, offering spectacular settings for day trips and adventures. These natural wonders provide opportunities for swimming, hiking, and enjoying the beauty of the Samoan landscape.

1. Papapapaitai Falls

Papapapaitai Falls, also known as Tiavi Falls, is one of the tallest waterfalls in Samoa, plunging over 100 meters into a deep gorge. Located in the central highlands of Upolu, this waterfall is a must-see for nature lovers.

- **Scenic Viewpoints:** The falls can be viewed from several lookout points along the Cross Island Road. These viewpoints offer breathtaking views of the waterfall and the surrounding rainforest.

- **Photography:** Papapapaitai Falls is a popular spot for photography due to its impressive height and picturesque setting. Early morning or late afternoon provides the best lighting for capturing the falls in their full glory.

2. Togitogiga Waterfall

Togitogiga Waterfall, located in O Le Pupu-Puʻe National Park on Upolu's south coast, is a beautiful spot for swimming and picnicking. The waterfall features multiple tiers and natural pools, creating a serene and inviting environment.

- **Swimming:** The pools at the base of the waterfall are perfect for swimming. The water is cool and refreshing, providing a welcome respite from the tropical heat.

- **Picnicking:** The area around Togitogiga Waterfall is equipped with picnic facilities, making it an ideal spot for a relaxing day out. Visitors can enjoy a meal surrounded by the natural beauty of the rainforest.

3. Afu Aau Waterfall

Afu Aau Waterfall, also known as Olemoe Falls, is located on the southern coast of Savai'i. This stunning waterfall cascades into a large, clear pool surrounded by lush vegetation.

- **Hiking:** A short hike through the forest leads to the waterfall, offering a chance to enjoy the island's flora and fauna. The trail is relatively easy and suitable for all fitness levels.

- **Swimming:** The pool at the base of Afu Aau Waterfall is perfect for swimming. The clear, cool water is incredibly inviting, and the surrounding rocks provide spots for sunbathing and relaxation.

- **Local Legends:** The waterfall is steeped in local legends, and visitors can learn about the cultural significance of the site from local guides. These stories add an extra layer of interest to the visit.

4. Sopoaga Waterfall

Sopoaga Waterfall, located in the village of Lotofaga on Upolu, is another beautiful spot for a day trip. The waterfall is set in a lush garden, providing a peaceful and picturesque setting.

- **Garden Walks:** The gardens around Sopoaga Waterfall are well-maintained and feature a variety of tropical plants and flowers. Visitors can enjoy a leisurely walk through the gardens while taking in the beauty of the waterfall.

- **Cultural Demonstrations:** The site often hosts cultural demonstrations, including traditional Samoan cooking and weaving. These demonstrations provide an opportunity to learn about Samoan culture and customs in a beautiful natural setting.

- **Picnicking:** The area is equipped with picnic facilities, making it a great spot to relax and enjoy a meal. The serene environment and the sound of the waterfall create a perfect backdrop for a peaceful afternoon.

5. Fuipisia Waterfall

Fuipisia Waterfall is located in the eastern part of Upolu and is known for its impressive height and beautiful surroundings. It offers a more secluded experience compared to some of the more popular waterfalls.

- **Viewpoints:** There are several viewpoints around Fuipisia Waterfall where visitors can take in the majestic sight of the water cascading down into the dense forest below. The viewpoints provide excellent photo opportunities.

- **Hiking:** A short hike through the lush landscape leads to the waterfall. The trail is relatively easy and offers a chance to see a variety of plant and bird species native to Samoa.

- **Tranquility:** The secluded nature of Fuipisia Waterfall means it is often less crowded, providing a tranquil environment for those seeking solitude and a deeper connection with nature.

Samoa offers an abundance of day trips and excursions that cater to a wide range of interests, from cultural immersion and historical exploration to outdoor adventures and relaxation in nature. Whether you are based in Apia and exploring the nearby attractions, venturing to the tranquil islands of Manono and Apolima, or seeking the thrill of discovering Samoa's stunning waterfalls, each experience promises to be enriching and unforgettable.

These excursions not only showcase the natural beauty and cultural heritage of Samoa but also provide opportunities for visitors to engage with the local communities, learn about their customs and traditions, and appreciate the island's unique charm. As you plan your travels, consider incorporating these day trips into your itinerary to fully experience the diverse and captivating aspects of Samoa.

Embrace the adventure, soak in the natural wonders, and immerse yourself in the vibrant culture of Samoa. Each excursion is a step closer to understanding the heart and soul of this beautiful island nation, leaving you with cherished memories and a deep appreciation for its people and landscapes.

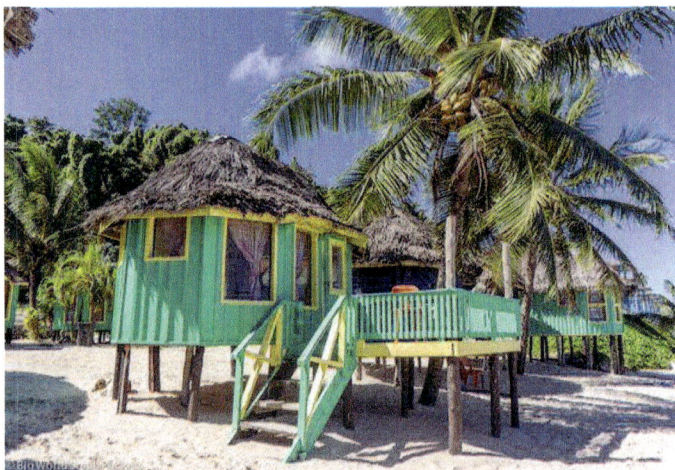

SAMPLE ITINERARIES

Creating an itinerary for a trip to Samoa can help you make the most of your time and ensure you experience the best the islands have to offer. Here are detailed sample itineraries for a 3-day, 5-day, and 7-day stay in Samoa, highlighting key attractions and activities to give you a well-rounded experience.

3-Day Itinerary: Highlights of Upolu

Day 1: Exploring Apia

- **Morning: Robert Louis Stevenson Museum**

    o Start your day with a visit to the Robert Louis Stevenson Museum. Take a guided tour to learn about the life and legacy of the famous author.

    o Stroll through the beautiful gardens and consider hiking to Stevenson's tomb on Mount Vaea for stunning views.

- **Afternoon: Apia's Markets and Cultural Village**

    o Head to Maketi Fou (the central market) to explore local produce, crafts, and souvenirs.

- o Visit the Samoa Cultural Village to experience traditional Samoan crafts, cooking, and dance performances.

- **Evening: Dinner in Apia**

  - o Enjoy dinner at Paddles Restaurant, known for its delicious seafood and Italian-inspired dishes.

  - o Take a leisurely evening walk along the waterfront to enjoy the sunset.

Day 2: South Coast Adventures

- **Morning: To Sua Ocean Trench**

  - o Drive to the south coast to visit the To Sua Ocean Trench. Swim in the crystal-clear waters and explore the surrounding gardens.

  - o Have a picnic lunch in one of the shaded areas around the trench.

- **Afternoon: Lalomanu Beach**

  - o Head to Lalomanu Beach, one of the most beautiful beaches in Samoa. Relax on the white sand, swim, and snorkel in the clear waters.

  - o Consider renting a beach fale for some shade and comfort.

- **Evening: Fiafia Night**

    o Return to your accommodation and participate in a fiafia night, where you can enjoy a traditional Samoan feast accompanied by cultural performances.

Day 3: Waterfalls and Coastal Views

- **Morning: Piula Cave Pool**

    o Visit Piula Cave Pool on the north coast for a refreshing swim in the natural freshwater pool.

    o Explore the historic Piula Theological College grounds.

- **Afternoon: Sopoaga and Togitogiga Waterfalls**

    o Travel to Sopoaga Waterfall for a leisurely garden walk and cultural demonstrations.

    o Continue to Togitogiga Waterfall in O Le Pupu-Puʻe National Park for a swim and picnic in a beautiful natural setting.

- **Evening: Relaxing Dinner**

    o Enjoy a relaxing dinner at Amanaki Restaurant in Apia, known for its delicious Samoan and international cuisine.

5-Day Itinerary: Upolu and Savai'i Exploration

Day 1: Arrival and Apia Highlights

- **Morning: Arrival and Check-in**

    o Arrive in Apia, check into your accommodation, and freshen up.

- **Afternoon: Robert Louis Stevenson Museum and Markets**

    o Visit the Robert Louis Stevenson Museum and explore Apia's markets.

- **Evening: Dinner in Apia**

    o Enjoy dinner at a local restaurant and explore Apia's nightlife.

Day 2: South Coast of Upolu

- **Morning: To Sua Ocean Trench**

    o Spend the morning at To Sua Ocean Trench, swimming and exploring.

- **Afternoon: Lalomanu Beach**

    o Relax at Lalomanu Beach, swim, snorkel, and enjoy a beach fale.

- Evening: Fiafia Night

  o Participate in a fiafia night at your accommodation.

Day 3: Transfer to Savai'i and Island Exploration

- Morning: Ferry to Savai'i

  o Take the ferry from Mulifanua Wharf on Upolu to Salelologa Wharf on Savai'i.

- Afternoon: Afu Aau Waterfall

  o Visit Afu Aau Waterfall for a swim in the clear pool surrounded by lush vegetation.

- Evening: Check-in and Relaxation

  o Check into your accommodation on Savai'i and enjoy a relaxing evening.

Day 4: Savai'i Adventures

- Morning: Saleaula Lava Fields

  o Explore the Saleaula Lava Fields and learn about the history of the volcanic eruption that created them.

- Afternoon: Alofaaga Blowholes

  o Visit the Alofaaga Blowholes to witness the powerful water geysers.

- **Evening: Beachfront Dinner**

  - Enjoy dinner at your beachside accommodation, taking in the stunning sunset views.

Day 5: Return to Upolu and Departure

- **Morning: Return Ferry to Upolu**

  - Take the morning ferry back to Upolu.

- **Afternoon: Last-Minute Shopping and Relaxation**

  - Spend the afternoon shopping for souvenirs and relaxing in Apia.

- **Evening: Departure**

  - Transfer to the airport for your departure flight.

7-Day Itinerary: In-Depth Samoa Experience

Day 1: Arrival and Apia Exploration

- **Morning: Arrival and Check-in**

  - Arrive in Apia, check into your accommodation, and freshen up.

- **Afternoon: Robert Louis Stevenson Museum**

    o Visit the Robert Louis Stevenson Museum and explore the surrounding gardens.

- **Evening: Dinner in Apia**

    o Enjoy dinner at a local restaurant and explore Apia's nightlife.

Day 2: South Coast and Beach Relaxation

- **Morning: To Sua Ocean Trench**

    o Spend the morning at To Sua Ocean Trench, swimming and exploring.

- **Afternoon: Lalomanu Beach**

    o Relax at Lalomanu Beach, swim, snorkel, and enjoy a beach fale.

- **Evening: Fiafia Night**

    o Participate in a fiafia night at your accommodation.

Day 3: North Coast and Piula Cave Pool

- **Morning: Piula Cave Pool**

    o Visit Piula Cave Pool for a refreshing swim and explore the college grounds.

- **Afternoon: Sopoaga Waterfall**
  - Travel to Sopoaga Waterfall for a garden walk and cultural demonstrations.
- **Evening: Dinner and Relaxation**
  - Return to Apia for dinner and a relaxing evening.

Day 4: Transfer to Savai'i and Island Exploration

- **Morning: Ferry to Savai'i**
  - Take the ferry from Mulifanua Wharf on Upolu to Salelologa Wharf on Savai'i.
- **Afternoon: Afu Aau Waterfall**
  - Visit Afu Aau Waterfall for a swim and explore the surrounding area.
- **Evening: Check-in and Relaxation**
  - Check into your accommodation on Savai'i and enjoy a relaxing evening.

Day 5: Savai'i Adventures

- **Morning: Saleaula Lava Fields**
  - Explore the Saleaula Lava Fields and learn about the volcanic history.

- Afternoon: Alofaaga Blowholes

  o Visit the Alofaaga Blowholes to witness the powerful water geysers.

- Evening: Beachfront Dinner

  o Enjoy dinner at your beachside accommodation, taking in the sunset.

Day 6: Manono Island Exploration

- Morning: Boat to Manono Island

  o Take a boat from Savai'i to Manono Island.

- Afternoon: Island Walk and Cultural Immersion

  o Explore the island on foot, visit traditional villages, and engage with the locals.

- Evening: Return to Savai'i

  o Return to Savai'i and enjoy a relaxing evening at your accommodation.

Day 7: Return to Upolu and Departure

- Morning: Return Ferry to Upolu

  o Take the morning ferry back to Upolu.

- Afternoon: Last-Minute Shopping and Relaxation

  o Spend the afternoon shopping for souvenirs and relaxing in Apia.

- **Evening: Departure**

    o Transfer to the airport for your departure
      flight.

These sample itineraries offer a comprehensive guide to
exploring Samoa, providing a mix of cultural experiences,
natural beauty, and relaxation. Whether you have a few days
or a week to spend in Samoa, these itineraries will help you
make the most of your trip and create unforgettable
memories.

PRACTICAL INFORMATION

Traveling to Samoa offers a chance to experience its stunning landscapes, vibrant culture, and warm hospitality. To ensure a smooth and enjoyable trip, it's essential to be prepared with practical information regarding health and safety, language and communication, electricity and connectivity, shopping and souvenirs, and tipping and etiquette. This guide provides detailed advice to help you make the most of your visit.

Health and Safety Tips

Health Precautions

- **Vaccinations:** While no specific vaccinations are required for entry into Samoa, it's recommended to be up-to-date on routine vaccines, such as measles, mumps, rubella (MMR), diphtheria-tetanus-pertussis, varicella (chickenpox), polio, and your annual flu shot. Additionally, consider vaccines for hepatitis A and B, typhoid, and tetanus, especially if you plan to explore rural areas or engage in outdoor activities.

- **Water and Food Safety:** Tap water in urban areas like Apia is generally safe to drink, but it's advisable to drink bottled or boiled water, especially in rural areas. Practice good food hygiene by eating well-cooked meals and avoiding raw or undercooked food from street vendors.

113

- **Mosquito Protection:** Mosquitoes in Samoa can carry diseases such as dengue fever and chikungunya. Protect yourself by using insect repellent, wearing long sleeves and pants, and staying in accommodations with screens or air conditioning.

Medical Services

- **Healthcare Facilities:** Samoa has several hospitals and clinics, with the main public hospital being the Tupua Tamasese Meaole Hospital in Apia. There are also private clinics that offer quality care. It's advisable to have comprehensive travel insurance that covers medical emergencies and evacuation, as more severe cases may require transfer to New Zealand or Australia.

- **Pharmacies:** Pharmacies are available in Apia and other major towns. It's wise to bring a supply of any prescription medications you need, as well as a basic first aid kit.

Safety Precautions

- **Personal Safety:** Samoa is generally safe, with low levels of crime. However, it's still important to take standard precautions, such as avoiding isolated areas at night, keeping valuables secure, and being aware of your surroundings.

- **Natural Disasters:** Samoa is prone to natural disasters such as cyclones and earthquakes. Familiarize yourself with local emergency procedures and stay informed about weather conditions during your stay. The cyclone season runs from November to April.

Language and Communication

Official Languages

- **Samoan:** The official language of Samoa is Samoan. It's widely spoken and used in everyday communication. Learning a few basic phrases in Samoan can enhance your travel experience and help you connect with locals.

  - Greetings: "Talofa" (Hello), "Fa'afetai" (Thank you)

  - Basic Phrases: "O a mai oe?" (How are you?), "Manuia le aso" (Have a nice day)

- **English:** English is also an official language and is commonly used in business, government, and tourism. Most Samoans are bilingual, so you should have no trouble communicating in English.

Communication Services

- **Internet and Wi-Fi:** Internet access is widely available in Samoa, particularly in urban areas and tourist accommodations. Many hotels, resorts, and cafes offer free Wi-Fi for guests. However, the speed and reliability of internet connections can vary.

- **Mobile Phones:** Local SIM cards can be purchased from major providers such as Digicel and Vodafone. These SIM cards offer affordable prepaid plans for calls, texts, and data. Ensure your phone is unlocked before purchasing a local SIM card.

- **Postal Services:** Samoa has reliable postal services, with post offices located in Apia and other major towns. International mail can be sent from these offices, and postal services are generally efficient.

Electricity and Connectivity

Electrical Standards

- **Voltage and Plugs:** Samoa uses a 230V supply voltage and 50Hz frequency. The standard socket type is Type I, which has three flat pins in a triangular pattern. If your devices use a different plug type or voltage, you will need an adapter or converter.

- **Power Outages:** While power outages are not common, they can occur, especially in rural areas. It's a good idea to have a flashlight and extra batteries on hand, and to charge your electronic devices when power is available.

Staying Connected

- **Internet Cafes:** In addition to Wi-Fi, internet cafes are available in Apia and other towns. These cafes provide a reliable connection and are a good option if you need to access the internet while exploring the islands.

- **Communication Apps:** Using communication apps such as WhatsApp, Skype, or Viber can be an effective way to stay in touch with family and friends back home. These apps require an internet connection but allow for free or low-cost calls and messages.

Shopping and Souvenirs

Local Markets and Shops

- **Maketi Fou (Central Market):** Located in Apia, Maketi Fou is the largest market in Samoa. It's a bustling hub where you can find fresh produce, traditional crafts, clothing, and souvenirs. It's an excellent place to immerse yourself in local culture and pick up unique items.

- **Fugalei Market:** Another popular market in Apia, Fugalei Market specializes in fresh fruits, vegetables, and local foods. It's a great place to try traditional Samoan snacks and purchase ingredients for a picnic or self-catering.

Traditional Crafts and Souvenirs

- **Siapo (Tapa Cloth):** Siapo is a traditional Samoan cloth made from the bark of the paper mulberry tree. It's decorated with intricate designs using natural dyes and is available in various forms, such as wall hangings, clothing, and accessories.

- **Wood Carvings:** Samoan artisans are known for their beautiful wood carvings, including kava bowls, walking sticks, and decorative items. These carvings often feature traditional patterns and symbols, making them meaningful souvenirs.

- **Weaving:** Woven items such as mats, baskets, and fans are common in Samoa. These items are made from pandanus leaves and are crafted with great skill and care.

- **Jewelry:** Shell and coconut jewelry are popular souvenirs. These pieces are often handmade and can include necklaces, bracelets, and earrings featuring local materials.

Shopping Tips

- **Bargaining:** Bargaining is not a common practice in Samoa. Prices are generally fixed, but you may be able to get a discount if you purchase multiple items from the same vendor.

- **Supporting Local Artisans:** Buying directly from local artisans and markets helps support the local economy and ensures that you are getting authentic, handmade items.

Tipping and Etiquette

Tipping

- **General Practice:** Tipping is not customary in Samoa, and service charges are usually included in the bill at hotels and restaurants. However, if you receive exceptional service, a small gratuity or a token of appreciation is always welcome.

- **Hotels and Restaurants:** While tipping is not expected, leaving a small amount for housekeeping staff or restaurant servers as a gesture of appreciation is a kind practice.

- **Tour Guides and Drivers:** If you have hired a tour guide or driver and they provided excellent service, a tip of around 10% of the total cost is appreciated but not obligatory.

Etiquette

- **Respect for Elders:** Samoan culture places a strong emphasis on respect for elders. When interacting with older individuals, show respect by addressing them politely and listening attentively.

- **Dress Code:** Samoa is a conservative society, and modest dress is appreciated, especially in villages and during church services. Avoid wearing revealing clothing, and cover your shoulders and knees when visiting cultural sites.

- **Greetings:** A warm handshake and a smile are common greetings in Samoa. When meeting someone for the first time, a polite "Talofa" (Hello) is appropriate.

- **Visiting Villages:** If you visit a traditional village, it's important to follow local customs. Always ask for permission before entering a fale (house) and remove your shoes before entering. Show respect by sitting quietly and waiting to be invited to speak.

Environmental Responsibility

- **Littering:** Samoa places a high value on cleanliness and environmental preservation. Dispose of trash properly and participate in recycling efforts whenever possible.

- **Marine Conservation:** When snorkeling or diving, avoid touching or standing on coral reefs. Coral is fragile and can be easily damaged. Respect marine life by observing from a distance and not removing any shells or marine organisms from their natural habitat.

Being well-prepared with practical information can significantly enhance your travel experience in Samoa. By taking health and safety precautions, understanding local customs and communication methods, ensuring you have the right electrical adapters, enjoying local shopping experiences, and respecting tipping and etiquette practices, you can fully immerse yourself in the beauty and culture of Samoa.

Embrace the warmth and hospitality of the Samoan people, explore the stunning landscapes, and create lasting memories in this island paradise. Whether you are visiting for a few days or an extended stay, the practical tips provided in this guide will help ensure a smooth, enjoyable, and respectful journey. Enjoy your time in Samoa, and let the natural beauty and rich culture of the islands leave a lasting impression on your heart and mind.

SUSTAINABLE TRAVEL

Traveling sustainably in Samoa not only helps preserve the pristine environment of this beautiful island nation but also supports the local communities and contributes to conservation efforts. By adopting eco-friendly practices, engaging with local initiatives, and participating in conservation projects, travelers can make a positive impact. This guide provides practical tips for sustainable travel, ways to support local communities, and opportunities for involvement in conservation projects.

Eco-Friendly Travel Tips

Traveling with an eco-conscious mindset helps minimize your environmental footprint and ensures that the natural beauty of Samoa is preserved for future generations. Here are some tips to help you travel sustainably:

1. Reduce Plastic Use

- **Bring Reusable Items:** Pack reusable water bottles, shopping bags, and containers to reduce your reliance on single-use plastics. Many hotels and guesthouses provide refill stations for water, making it easy to stay hydrated without using disposable bottles.

- **Avoid Plastic Packaging:** When shopping for snacks or souvenirs, choose items with minimal or no plastic packaging. Opt for fresh produce at local markets instead of pre-packaged goods.

2. Conserve Water and Energy

- **Be Mindful of Water Use:** Water is a precious resource on islands like Samoa. Take shorter showers, turn off the tap while brushing your teeth, and reuse towels when staying in accommodations.

- **Save Energy:** Turn off lights, air conditioning, and other electrical appliances when not in use. Consider staying in eco-friendly accommodations that implement energy-saving measures.

3. Choose Sustainable Transportation

- **Public Transport and Carpooling:** Use public transportation or carpool with other travelers to reduce carbon emissions. Buses in Samoa are not only eco-friendly but also offer a unique cultural experience.

- **Eco-Friendly Vehicles:** If renting a car, choose a fuel-efficient or hybrid vehicle. Alternatively, explore the islands by bicycle or on foot to reduce your environmental impact and enjoy the scenery up close.

4. Respect Wildlife and Natural Habitats

- **Observe from a Distance:** When encountering wildlife, maintain a respectful distance to avoid disturbing animals in their natural habitat. Avoid feeding or touching wildlife.

- **Stay on Trails:** Stick to marked trails when hiking to prevent damage to delicate ecosystems. Do not remove plants, rocks, or other natural items from their environment.

Supporting Local Communities

Engaging with and supporting local communities during your travels not only enriches your experience but also ensures that your spending benefits the people who call Samoa home. Here are some ways to support local communities:

1. Choose Local Accommodations

- **Stay in Locally Owned Lodges:** Opt for accommodations that are owned and operated by locals. This ensures that more of your money stays within the community and supports local jobs.

- **Experience Traditional Fales:** Staying in traditional beach fales offers a unique cultural experience and directly supports local families.

2. Eat Local

- **Dine at Local Restaurants:** Choose to eat at locally owned restaurants and food stalls instead of international chains. This supports local chefs and farmers and provides an authentic taste of Samoan cuisine.

- **Visit Markets:** Buy fresh produce and handmade goods from local markets. Engaging with vendors at markets like Maketi Fou helps sustain their livelihoods.

3. Shop Ethically

- **Buy Handcrafted Goods:** Purchase souvenirs and gifts that are handmade by local artisans. Items such as siapo (tapa cloth), wood carvings, and woven baskets are not only beautiful but also support traditional crafts.

- **Fair Trade Products:** Look for fair trade products that ensure fair wages and working conditions for producers.

4. Participate in Cultural Experiences

- **Join Cultural Tours:** Participate in tours and activities that are run by local guides. These experiences provide income for locals and offer deeper insights into Samoan culture and traditions.

- **Respect Traditions:** Show respect for local customs and traditions. Dress modestly, ask for permission before taking photos of people or private property, and learn a few phrases in Samoan to show your appreciation for the culture.

Conservation Projects and Volunteer Opportunities

Samoa is home to numerous conservation projects aimed at preserving its unique ecosystems and biodiversity. Participating in these initiatives allows travelers to give back to the environment and contribute to the sustainability of the islands.

1. Marine Conservation

- **Coral Reef Protection:** Engage with organizations that focus on coral reef conservation. Activities may include reef monitoring, coral planting, and education on sustainable fishing practices.

- **Beach Cleanups:** Join beach cleanup efforts to remove plastic and other debris from Samoa's shores. These activities help protect marine life and keep the beaches beautiful.

2. Forest Conservation

- **Tree Planting:** Participate in tree planting projects to help reforest areas that have been affected by deforestation. This helps restore habitats for wildlife and combat climate change.

- **Invasive Species Removal:** Volunteer with groups working to remove invasive plant species that threaten native biodiversity. This work is crucial for maintaining healthy ecosystems.

3. Wildlife Protection

- **Turtle Conservation:** Join programs that protect sea turtles, which are often threatened by poaching and habitat loss. Activities may include monitoring nesting sites, tagging turtles, and educating local communities.

- **Bird Watching and Research:** Assist with bird conservation projects that focus on protecting endemic and migratory bird species. This may involve conducting surveys, habitat restoration, and public awareness campaigns.

4. Community-Based Conservation

- **Eco-Tourism Initiatives:** Support eco-tourism projects that involve local communities in conservation efforts. These initiatives often combine environmental protection with sustainable development, benefiting both nature and people.

- **Education and Outreach:** Participate in educational programs that raise awareness about environmental issues among local communities and schools. This can include workshops, presentations, and hands-on activities.

Sustainable travel in Samoa is not only about preserving the environment but also about respecting and supporting the local culture and communities. By adopting eco-friendly practices, choosing to support local businesses, and participating in conservation projects, travelers can make a meaningful and positive impact on this beautiful island nation.

Embrace the opportunity to travel responsibly and immerse yourself in the rich culture and stunning natural landscapes of Samoa. Your efforts can help ensure that the pristine beaches, vibrant coral reefs, lush forests, and unique wildlife are preserved for future generations to enjoy. Whether you are exploring the islands, dining on local delicacies, or engaging in volunteer work, every action counts towards a more sustainable and respectful way of traveling.

Travel with a purpose, and let your journey in Samoa be a testament to the positive difference that conscious travelers can make. Enjoy the beauty of the islands, connect with the people, and leave a legacy of sustainability and respect.

TRAVELER RESOURCES

Traveling to Samoa is a delightful experience filled with stunning landscapes, vibrant culture, and warm hospitality. To ensure your trip is smooth and enjoyable, it's essential to have access to useful resources, contacts, and emergency numbers. This guide provides valuable information on useful contacts, travel apps and websites, and essential phrases to help you navigate and fully enjoy your time in Samoa.

Useful Contacts and Emergency Numbers

Being prepared with essential contacts and emergency numbers can provide peace of mind and ensure you have the necessary assistance if needed. Here are some important contacts and numbers to keep handy:

Emergency Services

- **General Emergency Number:** 911

  o This number connects you to emergency services, including police, fire, and medical assistance.

Medical Services

- **Tupua Tamasese Meaole Hospital (Apia):**

  o Phone: +685 21212

- o The main public hospital in Samoa, offering comprehensive medical services.

- **MedCen Hospital (Private Hospital, Apia):**

  - o Phone: +685 32032

  - o A private hospital providing a range of medical services and emergency care.

Police Stations

- **Central Police Station (Apia):**

  - o Phone: +685 22222

  - o For non-emergency police assistance and inquiries.

- **Faleolo Police Station (Near Airport):**

  - o Phone: +685 44444

  - o Located near Faleolo International Airport for airport-related inquiries and assistance.

Embassies and Consulates

- **Australian High Commission:**

  - o Phone: +685 23411

- **New Zealand High Commission:**

  - o Phone: +685 21711

- **United States Embassy:**

  o Phone: +685 21436

Tourism Information

- **Samoa Tourism Authority (Apia):**

  o Phone: +685 63500

  o Website: www.samoa.travel

  o Provides information on tourist attractions, accommodations, and travel tips.

Travel Apps and Websites

Leveraging technology can enhance your travel experience by providing useful information, maps, and services at your fingertips. Here are some recommended travel apps and websites:

Travel Apps

- **Google Maps:** Essential for navigation and finding directions to various attractions, accommodations, and restaurants in Samoa.

- **XE Currency Converter:** Helps you keep track of currency exchange rates and convert prices to your home currency.

- **TripIt:** Organizes your travel itinerary, including flight details, accommodation bookings, and activities.

- **Maps.me:** An offline map app that allows you to download maps of Samoa and use them without an internet connection, handy for exploring remote areas.

- **WhatsApp:** A widely used messaging app that allows you to stay connected with family and friends through text, voice, and video calls using an internet connection.

Travel Websites

- **Samoa Tourism Authority:** www.samoa.travel

  o Official tourism website providing comprehensive information on attractions, accommodations, events, and travel tips.

- **Airbnb:** www.airbnb.com

  o A platform for booking unique accommodations, including local homes and guesthouses.

- **Booking.com:** www.booking.com

  o Offers a wide range of accommodations from hotels to guesthouses with user reviews and detailed descriptions.

- **TripAdvisor:** www.tripadvisor.com
  - o Provides reviews and recommendations for hotels, restaurants, and attractions, helping you make informed travel decisions.

Useful Phrases

Learning a few basic phrases in Samoan can enhance your travel experience and help you connect with locals. Here are some useful phrases to know:

Greetings and Common Phrases

- **Hello:** Talofa
- **Goodbye:** Tofa
- **Please:** Fa'amolemole
- **Thank you:** Fa'afetai
- **Yes:** Ioe
- **No:** Leai
- **Excuse me/Sorry:** Fa'amalie atu
- **How are you?:** O a mai oe?
- **I am fine:** Manuia fa'afetai

Directions and Assistance

- **Where is the bathroom?:** O fea le faleta'ele?

- **Can you help me?:** E mafai ona e fesoasoani mai?

- **I need a doctor:** Ou te mana'omia se foma'i

- **Where is...?:** O fea le...?

    o (For example: O fea le maketi? - Where is the market?)

Shopping and Dining

- **How much is this?:** E fia le tau o lenei?

- **I would like...:** Ou te fia...

    o (For example: Ou te fia inu - I would like a drink)

- **Water:** Vai

- **Food:** Mea'ai

- **Delicious:** Manaia

- **Bill, please:** Fa'amolemole, aumai le pili

Cultural Respect

- **Beautiful:** Matagofie

- **My name is...:** O lo'u igoa o...

- **Nice to meet you:** Ua ou fiafia ua ta feiloa'i

- **Excuse me (to pass by):** Tulou lava

Having access to useful contacts, reliable travel apps and websites, and knowing some essential phrases can significantly enhance your travel experience in Samoa. By being prepared and equipped with this practical information, you can ensure a smooth, enjoyable, and respectful visit to this beautiful island nation.

Whether you are exploring the vibrant markets of Apia, relaxing on the pristine beaches, or immersing yourself in the rich cultural heritage of Samoa, these resources will help you make the most of your journey. Embrace the adventure, connect with the local people, and create lasting memories in Samoa.

CONCLUSION

As I sit on the sandy shores of Lalomanu Beach, watching the sun dip below the horizon and listening to the gentle rhythm of the waves, I can't help but reflect on the incredible journey I've experienced in Samoa. This trip has been more than just a vacation; it has been an immersion into a world where nature's beauty and cultural richness are harmoniously intertwined. Each day brought new adventures and profound connections that left an indelible mark on my heart.

My travels began in Apia, the bustling capital, where the vibrant energy of the markets and the warmth of the people immediately made me feel at home. Visiting the Robert Louis Stevenson Museum was a highlight, as I walked through the very rooms where the famous author found inspiration and solace. The gardens surrounding the museum provided a peaceful retreat, and the hike to his tomb on Mount Vaea offered stunning views that reminded me of the island's breathtaking landscapes.

The south coast of Upolu was a haven of tranquility. Swimming in the To Sua Ocean Trench, I felt a sense of awe and gratitude for the natural wonders of this world. Lalomanu Beach, with its powdery white sand and crystal-clear waters, was the perfect spot to unwind and appreciate the simple joys of life. The traditional beach fales offered a unique and authentic experience, connecting me even more deeply with the Samoan way of life.

Exploring the islands of Manono and Apolima was like stepping back in time. On Manono Island, I was welcomed into the community, learning about their traditions and way of life. Walking around the island, I marveled at the untouched beauty and felt a profound respect for the people who live in harmony with nature. Apolima, with its rugged landscapes and close-knit community, offered a quiet retreat that felt like a hidden gem waiting to be discovered.

My journey through Samoa wouldn't have been complete without the adventure of exploring its majestic waterfalls. From the towering Papapapaitai Falls to the serene Afu Aau Waterfall, each site was a testament to the island's natural splendor. Swimming in the cool, clear pools and listening to the roar of the falls was a rejuvenating experience that connected me with the raw power of nature.

Throughout my travels, I made a conscious effort to embrace sustainable practices. I carried reusable items, conserved water and energy, and supported local businesses. Engaging with conservation projects and participating in community-based tourism initiatives allowed me to give back to the environment and the people who had welcomed me so warmly. The pride and passion of the Samoan people in preserving their heritage and natural beauty inspired me to travel more responsibly and mindfully.

Learning a few phrases in Samoan not only helped me communicate more effectively but also showed my respect for the local culture. Simple greetings and expressions of gratitude opened doors to deeper connections and memorable interactions. The smiles and warmth I received in return were priceless and reminded me of the universal language of kindness.

As my time in Samoa comes to an end, I realize that this journey has been about more than just seeing new places. It has been about embracing a different way of life, one that values community, tradition, and the natural world. The lessons I've learned here will stay with me long after I leave these shores. Samoa has taught me the importance of sustainable travel, the joy of cultural immersion, and the beauty of living in harmony with nature.

I leave Samoa with a heart full of gratitude and memories that will last a lifetime. This island paradise has not only given me unforgettable experiences but has also enriched my soul. As I prepare to board my flight back home, I carry with me the spirit of fa'a Samoa—the Samoan way of life—and the hope that I can return one day to this beautiful place that has become a part of me.

Thank you, Samoa, for sharing your beauty, culture, and hospitality. You have touched my heart and inspired me to be a better traveler and a more mindful steward of this precious planet. Until we meet again, fa'afetai lava and tofa soifua.

FAQs

1. What is the best time to visit Samoa?

The best time to visit Samoa is during the dry season, which runs from May to October. During this period, the weather is generally sunny and pleasant, making it ideal for outdoor activities, beach outings, and exploring the islands. The wet season, from November to April, can bring heavy rains and occasional cyclones, but it also means fewer tourists and lush green landscapes.

2. Do I need a visa to travel to Samoa?

Visa requirements for Samoa vary depending on your nationality. Many travelers from countries such as Australia, New Zealand, the United States, and most European countries can enter Samoa without a visa for stays up to 60 days. However, it's always best to check with the Samoan consulate or embassy in your country for the latest visa requirements and regulations.

3. How can I get around the islands?

Samoa has several transportation options:

- **Buses:** Public buses are an affordable way to travel around the islands, though they do not follow strict schedules.

- **Taxis:** Taxis are widely available, especially in Apia and other towns. It's advisable to agree on the fare before starting your journey.

- **Rental Cars:** Renting a car is a convenient option for exploring at your own pace. Remember to drive on the left side of the road.

- **Ferries:** Regular ferry services operate between the main islands of Upolu and Savai'i, making inter-island travel straightforward.

4. What should I pack for my trip to Samoa?

When packing for Samoa, consider the tropical climate and cultural norms:

- **Lightweight Clothing:** Breathable, lightweight clothes for warm weather.

- **Swimwear:** For beaches and swimming pools.

- **Modest Clothing:** For visiting villages and cultural sites.

- **Sun Protection:** Sunscreen, hats, and sunglasses.

- **Insect Repellent:** To protect against mosquitoes.

- **Comfortable Footwear:** For walking and outdoor activities.

- **Reusable Water Bottle:** To stay hydrated and reduce plastic waste.

5. Is it safe to travel to Samoa?

Samoa is generally a safe destination for travelers. However, it's always wise to take standard precautions:

- **Personal Safety:** Avoid isolated areas at night, secure your valuables, and stay aware of your surroundings.

- **Health Precautions:** Drink bottled or boiled water, use insect repellent, and ensure you have comprehensive travel insurance.

6. What currency is used in Samoa, and are credit cards widely accepted?

The currency used in Samoa is the Samoan Tala (WST). Credit cards are accepted in most hotels, restaurants, and larger shops, especially in Apia. However, it's advisable to carry some cash, particularly when visiting rural areas and smaller establishments. ATMs are available in Apia and other major towns.

7. What language is spoken in Samoa, and will I have trouble communicating?

The official languages of Samoa are Samoan and English. English is widely spoken, especially in tourist areas, making communication relatively easy for English-speaking travelers. Learning a few basic phrases in Samoan can enhance your experience and help you connect with locals.

8. What are some must-see attractions in Samoa?

Some must-see attractions in Samoa include:

- **To Sua Ocean Trench:** A stunning natural swimming hole.

- **Robert Louis Stevenson Museum:** The former home of the famous author.

- **Lalomanu Beach:** Known for its beautiful white sand and clear waters.

- **Alofaaga Blowholes:** Spectacular natural water spouts.

- **Papapapaitai Falls:** One of the tallest waterfalls in Samoa.

9. How can I support sustainable tourism in Samoa?

Supporting sustainable tourism in Samoa involves:

- **Reducing Plastic Use:** Bring reusable items and avoid single-use plastics.

- **Supporting Local Businesses:** Stay in locally owned accommodations, eat at local restaurants, and buy handmade crafts.

- **Conserving Resources:** Be mindful of water and energy use.

- **Participating in Conservation Projects:** Join local conservation efforts and volunteer opportunities.

10. What is the tipping policy in Samoa?

Tipping is not customary in Samoa, and service charges are usually included in the bill at hotels and restaurants. However, if you receive exceptional service, leaving a small gratuity as a token of appreciation is always welcome. Tipping tour guides and drivers for excellent service is also appreciated but not obligatory.

11. What cultural etiquette should I be aware of when visiting Samoa?

When visiting Samoa, it's important to respect local customs and traditions:

- **Dress Modestly:** Especially in villages and during church services. Cover shoulders and knees.

- **Show Respect:** Address elders politely and listen attentively.

- **Remove Shoes:** Before entering a fale (house) or a church.

- **Avoid Public Displays of Affection:** As they may be considered inappropriate.

12. Are there any special events or festivals I should try to attend?

Samoa hosts several vibrant festivals throughout the year:

- **Teuila Festival:** Held in the first week of September, showcasing Samoan culture through dance, music, and arts.

- **Independence Day:** Celebrated on June 1st with parades, ceremonies, and festivities.

- **Fire Knife Dance Competitions:** Exciting events featuring traditional Samoan fire knife dancing.

13. What kind of food can I expect to find in Samoa?

Samoan cuisine features fresh, locally sourced ingredients and traditional cooking methods:

- **Oka:** Raw fish marinated in lemon juice and coconut cream.

- **Palusami:** Taro leaves filled with coconut cream and baked.

- **Umu-Cooked Foods:** Meals cooked in an earth oven, including fish, pork, and root vegetables.

Enjoying local food at markets and restaurants provides an authentic taste of Samoan culture.

Traveling to Samoa is an enriching experience that combines natural beauty, cultural immersion, and warm hospitality. By being well-prepared with practical information and respecting local customs, you can ensure a memorable and enjoyable visit.

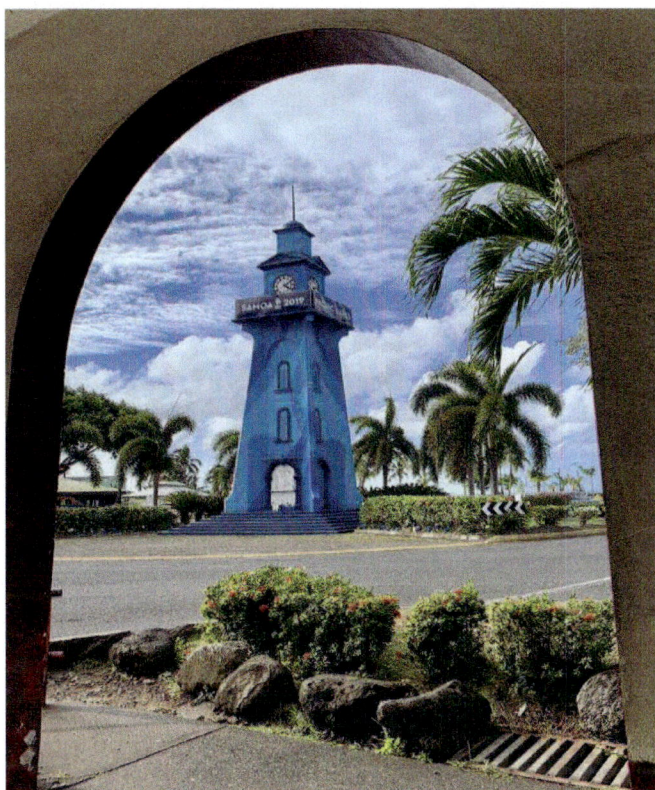

Printed in Great Britain
by Amazon